Praise for
Lovina's Song

"This book is educational and exciting...a wonderful blend of historical fact with a touch of fiction."

TODAY'S LIBRARIAN Magazine

"*Lovina's Song* is full of the personal touches that bring alive the trials of setting out to build a new life in the California of the 1840's. Surrounded by her extended family, young Lovina Graves is captivated by the adventure that awaits them.

What unfolds is a story of courage, tragedy and triumph as Lovina and her family join the ill-fated Donner Party. Vividly told and filled with the historical detail of everyday life, *Lovina's Song* is destined to become a much-loved volume in the young reader's library."

DR. VIRGINIA RUE
Assistant Superintendent of Schools
Instructional Support Services
Napa Valley Unified School District
Napa, California

"...really augments the 4th and 5th grade curriculum, while being absorbing as historical fiction. Doesn't 'talk down' to intermediate students in reading level on some of the sensitive subject matter."

JILL BRACKMAN
4th and 5th Grade School Teacher
Elk Grove Unified School District
Sacramento, California

"What a delightful tale, inspired by local history and true to life's experience. This is historical fiction that children will love and teachers will appreciate as a valuable resource."

DR. OLIVE MCARDLE-KULAS
Director, K–Adult Curriculum
Napa Valley Unified School District
Napa, California

What gift has Providence bestowed on man that is so dear to him as his children?
– Cicero

LOVINA'S SONG

LOVINA'S SONG

A
Pioneer Girl's
Journey
with the
Donner Party

MARIAN RUDOLPH

Citron Bay
P R E S S

Lovina's Song
A Pioneer Girl's Journey with the Donner Party
© Copyright 1999 by Marian Rudolph
Second Printing

Published by
Citron Bay Press
Marin County, California
www.citronbay.com

Library of Congress Catalog Card Number 99-61583
ISBN 1-928595-01-4

Book designed by Michael Saint James
Cover art and illustrations by Christopher Cole

Dedication

To my daughter Becky and my
granddaughters Amy and Megan,
without whose encouragement this
story would not have been told.

Acknowledgments

I know how much the support of friends and family mean to a fledgling writer. I have likened this project to an extended pregnancy, but I'm afraid only an elephant has such a long and cumbersome gestation.

My heartfelt thanks to my good friends Sharon Elwell, Reg Harris, Ginny Heitz, Anne, Monica and Margaret Nissen, Pat Williams, Wendy Cole and Terry Faherty for their encouragement and help.

My undying gratitude goes also to my dear husband, Ross, for his patience and understanding during the long days and nights with only the back of my head for company as I labored at the keyboard.

I am especially grateful to Mildred Hagstrom, Lovina's great-granddaughter, Lucy and Bill Kortum and Maxine Kortum Durney, Sarah's great-grandchildren, for their editing help, historical expertise and permission to use family references.

In reading stories about the Donner journey, I found many differing opinions as to the actual dates, places, and names of the people involved. It therefore became necessary for me to make choices concerning some of the events and personalities, to make them fit my tale. I hope I have not offended any serious historians or the descendants of the Donner families.

Any errors are my own. My intention has not been to make this a historical treatise, but rather to write a story about events as they might have been seen through the eyes of an eleven-year-old girl. Without the useful information and advice of my friend Kristen Johnson and her book, *Unfortunate Emigrants*, it would have been impossible for me to learn what I needed to tell the story from Lovina's point of view.

My deepest thanks to everyone who helped me birth this book.

Table of Contents

Prologue

Emmy began to hurry as she heard her grandmother softly playing the old piano in the parlor. "I'm almost finished with the dishes, Grandma," she called from the kitchen. "Let's sing *Home Sweet Home* today." It was her Grandmother's favorite.

Emmy had come to the Napa Valley to spend a few weeks with her grandmother during the summer, and she loved the hours they spent sitting at the piano, laughing and trying to remember the words to old familiar tunes.

"Well, hurry along, dear. We have work to do in the garden this afternoon, too," called her grandmother.

Emmy's real name was Edna Maybelle, but everyone called her by her family nickname. She quite liked it, in fact. Edna Maybelle Sherwood sounded so...well, so serious.

Emmy loved it here on the farm where she could poke around the big barn and look at all the interesting things in this comfortable old house. It was different from her own home in San Francisco, where everything was noisy and crowded and everyone was hurrying here and there.

Country life was quiet, and there were wonderful places for her to explore: the closets, the bookshelves, and especially the attic. She knew there must be stories hidden everywhere in the old books, pictures and boxes she found.

Grandma was a wonderful storyteller. Emmy liked hearing her animal tales and stories about the early days in the valley. But there was one part of her grandmother's life she never talked about, and of course that was just the story Emmy most wanted to hear.

Everyone knew about those poor immigrants who had been caught in the mountains with the Donner Party that terrible winter so long ago, and she knew her grandmother's family had been with them, but her grandmother had never spoken of it and Emmy couldn't help wondering why.

When she finished putting away the lunch dishes, she hung the towel on the rack next to the big wood stove and hurried into the parlor. She looked at her grandmother's sweet face and smiling blue eyes and wondered again about the sights those eyes had seen. Maybe today she'd find the courage to ask…did she dare?

"Grandma?" Emmy slipped onto the piano bench beside her grandmother.

"Yes, dear?"

"You've been here in the valley a long time, haven't you?"

Grandmother stopped playing and put her arm around Emmy's shoulders. "Goodness gracious, child, I surely have, but you know all about that. Now tell me, is something bothering you, dear? I've had the feeling all week that you have something on your mind."

Emmy looked down at her hands.

"Oh, it's just the kids at school, Grandma. They're always talking about me behind my back, or teasing me about my family."

"Why, honey, whatever for?"

"Well…" Emmy hesitated. "It's about the Donner Party. I've told them that my family came west in the covered wagons and now they want to know if those awful stories are true. Were those people really so hungry they…?" She couldn't go on.

"Oh, my dear Emmy," Grandmother shook her head. "I had hoped by now people would have forgotten all that."

"Oh, no! The kids at school talk about it all the time in our history class. I just don't know what to tell them."

Her grandmother hesitated. She closed her eyes and let her mind wander back. The events of that year filled everyone with such curiosity. Many people had asked her to talk about their terrible journey, but she always refused.

She'd rather leave it all behind her. But she knew that Emmy and her friends were curious about the Donner Party stories. Maybe she should try to tell Emmy what she could remember. She deserves to know her family's story, she thought. And as difficult as it would be, maybe…well maybe she needed to go back to those times herself.

Their ordeal seemed unreal, even to her, and each survivor had a different story to tell. To hear some of them talk, she wondered if they had all made the same trip!

It's been a long time, she thought. I was little more than a child myself. Her eyes clouded over as she looked out of the window to the big oak tree in the front yard, its broad bower of leaves offering welcoming shade from the warm summer sun, and thought back to her childhood, to her family and their fateful journey to this beautiful valley.

She took her granddaughter's hands in hers and looked into her eyes. "I thought when we got to California that dreadful trip was behind us, honey, but I guess the memories will always be there. Would you like me to tell you about it?"

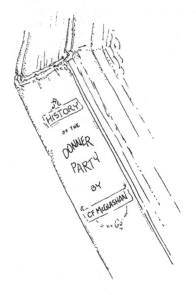

"Oh, yes, Grandma, please do."

"Remember, I was just a girl then. I may not get it all right."

"That's all right, Grandma. Just tell me what you can remember."

"Well…all right, honey. I guess our gardening can wait. I'll make some lemonade and we can sit out on the porch."

Emmy jumped up and ran to open the door for her grandmother. At last she was going to hear the real story! Maybe now she'd have some answers for her friends.

As they settled down, cool lemonade in hand, Grandmother slowly began rocking the old porch swing back and forth.

"It was the spring of 1846 when we began hearing about California. It was all anyone talked about—this wonderful new land out west, not even a state yet. Your grandfather's family and mine were among the first emigrants to come here to the Napa Valley, you know.

"My folks were living in Marshall County, Illinois, back then, and they were excited to think about moving out to California: the sunshine, the opportunities, the adventure.

"I was just about your age and I wasn't so sure I wanted to go at first. It did seem like a grand idea: wagons of friends and family, all traveling together to this new land, but I wasn't so sure I wanted to leave the only home I'd ever known.

"It was a long time ago, Emmy." She shook her head. "And my name wasn't Lovina Cyrus then. I was just Lovina Graves, 11 years old, with no idea what my future would hold. No one could have guessed what lay ahead of us."

1

Early Spring

1846
Marshall County, Illinois

Lovina huddled near the edge of the loft with her arms wrapped tightly around her knees, listening intently to the conversation coming from the kitchen below. Sure that her parents didn't want her eavesdropping, she strained to hear all that was said, without daring to venture down where she could hear better.

"There's good land free for the askin'! And it's sunny and warm, even in the winter! They say you can grow almost anything out there. There's game aplenty and friends already gone on ahead. Why, folks say it's a Garden of Eden, Elizabeth."

It was her father speaking, pleading his case to pack up all of their worldly belongings and set off for California. Father had never been much of a farmer, and Lovina knew his love of hunting and fishing was really what was drawing him west. She also knew her mother would be more easily convinced if he could paint a picture of good farmland and a warm home for her and the children.

Her mother's voice was too soft to be heard clearly, but Vine, as her family often called her, knew what her mother would be saying, "Oh, Franklin…the children's schooling…it's so far away…don't know if we could make such a long journey…so many little ones."

She knew her mother's greatest worry was her family. How could they just pick up and leave with so many children? It was hard enough to feed and clothe them here on the farm. How would they manage out on the plains?

Lovina had heard these arguments many times before. She wasn't sure what she wanted them to do. She was glad she wasn't the one to have to make the decision.

"Now, Elizabeth," she heard her father continue, "we don't have to decide tonight, but we can't wait too much longer. This cold snap we've been havin' will be over soon, and folks around here are makin' plans. If we start by the first of April, we should have plenty of time to make it over the mountains before the winter snows set in."

The rest of the family could hardly wait to be on their way. One after another they pleaded with her, "Oh, Mama, think how wonderful it'll be to have a winter with no snow. We'll be able to grow our crops and not worry about whether there'll be enough to last us through the year. Why, we could even have a flower garden!"

Lovina loved her big family. Besides her mother and father, there were nine children. Sarah, the eldest, was twenty-two and recently married. She had always been the quiet and serious one of the family. Lovina knew she would never encourage them to do anything foolish.

Next came Mary, two years younger. Everyone agreed she was the family beauty and would surely be the next to marry. She and Sarah had been secretly trying to decide which of Mary's many boyfriends she should choose as a husband. Lovina thought they were pretty silly. She wasn't going to get married for a long, long time—maybe never!

Eighteen-year-old Will was next. He was the oldest boy, and Father would expect him to be his helper on the trip, but Will was beginning to have a mind of his own. Lovina wondered how he and Father would get along on such a long journey.

Eleanor, or Ellen as her family called her, was nearly fourteen, three years older than Vine, and her best friend. They looked more alike than the others, with their father's clear blue eyes and curly brown hair. Ellen was slender and pretty, just beginning to be noticed by the young men of Marshall County. Vine knew that her sister was going to love the excitement of this new adventure.

And then came Lovina, eleven years old, the middle child, and the official family worrier.

Next were the four younger children: Nancy, 9, Jonathan, 7, Franklin Jr., 5, and baby Elizabeth, who wasn't yet a year old.

Everyone thought it would be fun to meet new people and to settle in this paradise that lay on the far western edge of the continent. Lovina and her mother weren't so sure.

Sarah and Jay Fosdick were anxious to settle down out West. They were staying in Sarah's old room. Lovina could hear Jay telling her sister about the plans he had for them when they got to California. "Oh, Sarah, it's gonna be somethin'! We'll build us a house and start a family. It'll be wonderful. Just you wait and see."

In some ways this new adventure did sound exciting to Lovina, but she hated to think of leaving Illinois, where she had everything she loved: her friends, her teacher, and especially the piano.

Lovina had been taking lessons from her mother's elderly Aunt Mary for almost a year, and she had such fun playing her favorite songs on the handsome old upright in her great-aunt's parlor. She'd been working for months to learn *Home Sweet Home*, and her heart was set on playing it at the recital next fall. But of course the piano would have to stay behind, along with all of her music.

Home Sweet Home was her favorite! The words were so lovely:

> *'Mid pleasures and palaces,*
> *Though we may roam,*
> *Be it ever so humble,*
> *There's no place like home.*

Her mind raced with questions: Could there ever be any place like her home right here in Marshall County? And what about those terrifying stories they'd heard about fierce Indians out west? What if someone traveling ahead made them angry and they were on the warpath? She'd heard lots of tales about wild Indian attacks.

"No," Lovina decided, "I don't think the West is for me."

But by the end of March, the decision was made. They were going! Four families would make up their party, with nine wagons in all.

Father found a buyer for the farm and a whirlwind of

activity began. The last few weeks flew by as her father and Jay hurried to build their three wagons and scouted around for another driver.

There were signs posted all around:

WESTWARD HO FOR CALIFORNIA
WHO WANTS TO GO TO CALIFORNIA WITHOUT COSTING THEM ANYTHING?

WANTED: MEN OF GOOD CHARACTER WHO CAN DRIVE AN OX TEAM.
THE GOVERNMENT OF CALIFORNIA IS GIVING LARGE TRACTS OF LAND TO HER SONS WHO MOVE HERE.

Young John Snyder was anxious to earn his way west and eagerly joined the Graves family as the preparations began.

Mother and the older girls spent days sorting and packing, trying to decide what to take with them and what to leave behind. Everywhere Lovina turned people were bustling. Mother had jobs for everyone.

"Come, Vine, give me a hand with this trunk."

"Oh dear, do we have to leave Grandma's good china behind?"

"Don't forget to pack those quilts and the woolen blankets!"

"Books? Well, I guess we can spare room for a few in that old trunk there. Be sure to pack the Bible carefully."

"Have you packed the plates and cups, Ellen, and the cooking utensils? Be sure to wrap them tightly. Have to keep the dirt out."

"Let's see now, beans, rice, coffee, dried meat, cornmeal. Are we sure we have enough of everything?"

Father had his say, too. "You youngsters understand you'll be walkin' most of the way now, don't you? These oxen have enough to pull with all the things you women have insisted on bringin' along." He was reminding them that they would have to be responsible for themselves on this long trip.

As the final decisions were made, the wagons were loaded with their carefully chosen belongings. Lovina found herself caught up in the packing, and soon she, too, began to look forward to their new adventure.

The air was filled with anticipation. Although the younger children ran and played, the others were busy with a thousand things.

EARLY SPRING

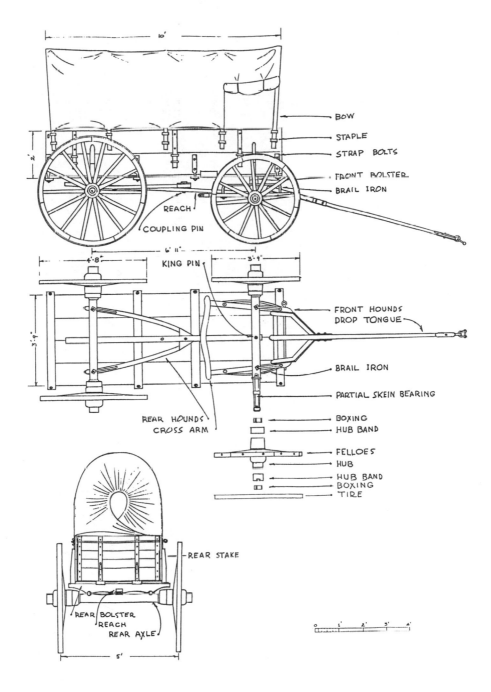

BOW
STAPLE
STRAP BOLTS
FRONT BOLSTER
BRAIL IRON
REACH
COUPLING PIN

10'
2'

KING PIN
6' 11"
4'-8"
3'-9"
3'-9"

FRONT HOUNDS
DROP TONGUE

BRAIL IRON
PARTIAL SKEIN BEARING
BOXING
HUB BAND
FELLOES
HUB
HUB BAND
BOXING
TIRE

REAR HOUNDS
CROSS ARM

REAR STAKE

REAR BOLSTER
REACH
REAR AXLE

5'

0 1' 2' 3' 4'

15

2

Off We Go

At last they were ready. The big day of departure finally arrived. The family dogs barked wildly as the drivers hitched up the oxen and tied the two riding horses they were bringing with them to the last wagon. Even the cows milling about seemed to know they too would be joining this noisy crowd. Friends and neighbors, anxious to say a last good-bye, gathered to see them off and wish them well.

The drivers cracked their whips and called out a loud, "Gee! Haw there!" The oxen leaned against their yokes and the wagons eased ahead, wheels creaking noisily as they moved slowly out onto the smooth dirt road leaving town. The long journey had begun.

Though there were tears on the faces of most of the older people, the younger children giggled and ran ahead as if they were leaving on a summer picnic.

"I don't think they have any idea what's up ahead," said Ellen.

"Do any of us?" wondered Lovina.

Father walked along with the first of the family wagons. Mother rode inside with baby Elizabeth. John Snyder followed with the second, and Jay's wagon brought up the rear. The older children rode on the family saddle horses and Lovina and Ellen walked with Sarah, next to Jay's team. The rest of the children were scattered between the first two rigs.

"Oh, Vine, I can't believe we're really on our way! I

didn't think this morning would ever come! Aren't you excited?" Ellen could hardly keep still.

Lovina didn't answer her sister. She was waving a long, tearful good-bye to Aunt Mary, already getting smaller in the distance. Would she ever see her or the piano again?

"Sarah," she asked finally, "Do you think we'll come back to Marshall County some day?"

Sarah put her arms around the girls and gave them a hug, but the serious look on her face told them that this wasn't the time for such questions.

Lovina and Ellen had always talked together about every-thing, sharing their secret hopes and fears, but Sarah wouldn't listen to any foolish talk. They were on their way now. There was no turning back.

The weather was warm and pleasant for the first few days, but there were places where the road was deep with muddy ruts, a reminder that many wagons had passed through during the recent spring rains.

The roads soon began to dry out however, and the mud turned to dust so thick they could hardly breathe.

"Slow down, boys," Father ordered. "Let's put some dis-tance between these wagons. Maybe some of this dust will settle if we're not so close."

"I can't even see the rest of the wagons, and I have a mouthful of sand," complained Ellen. "This trip isn't as much fun as I thought it was going to be."

"It'll be better soon," promised Jay. "I think I see a stream up ahead. We can get some water and clean up."

"Oh, a bath sounds wonderful!" Lovina cried, and began to run ahead.

When they reached the stream, the air was black with swarms of mosquitoes. Soon every inch of bare skin was covered with red itchy bites.

"Keep yourselves covered," Mother ordered. "Those

wild onions
and
watercress

skeeters are bothersome, but they won't hurt you. Just try not to scratch."

"Here, let me put some of this mud on you, Vine," said Ellen. "Sarah says it helps stop the itching." A bath was impossible.

The days went by slowly at first, but they soon began to overtake other trains of wagons headed west. Most had children with them, and though there wasn't much time for playing, the Graves children were happy to make new friends.

"Look, Jonathan," Will called one day, "wild turkeys! Shall we shoot one, Dad?"

"Sounds like a good idea to me," said his father. "Mother can roast it over the fire this afternoon." The early stop was welcomed by everyone.

The men hunted for birds and small game while the children picked wild onions and watercress to eat with the turkey for their evening meal.

The nights were still cool this early in the year and their warm bedding felt good as they settled down on the soft grass under their wagon.

"Night, Vine," said Ellen.

"Night, Ellen." Lovina smiled as she settled down for the night. Her stomach was full, the sky was bright with stars and their journey was going well. She wondered what new sights tomorrow would bring.

Morning dawned bright and clear the next day, and as soon as they broke camp and hitched up the animals, they were on their way again.

The older girls took turns tending baby Elizabeth in the back of the wagon while Mother walked along with the others. Father's twinkling blue eyes and good-natured grin always made their mother smile as she watched him coax the plodding oxen over the uneven roads.

Like many of the emigrants, Franklin Graves was a frontiersman. He loved wild country and he didn't mind hard work. But he didn't have much experience in handling the big oxen and found them hard to maneuver.

He had chosen oxen over horses or mules to pull the wagons because they were stronger, and though they were slower, they were less likely to be driven off by Indians during the night.

The Illinois River was near the Graves home in Marshall County, so the children had seen many boats that were used to carry goods between the small towns and villages nearby. Smaller boats were paddled, but many of the larger barges were poled across. When Lovina saw the great Mississippi stretched out ahead of them she couldn't believe her eyes. She had never seen a river so wide and it frightened her. How would they ever get to the other side?

"Now don't you worry," said her father. "We'll hire us some boatmen to take us over, but we've got work to do."

The wagons had to be taken apart and loaded onto the barges before they could be ferried across. The wide, slow-moving river carried them downstream to the landing on the other side, where the entire rig and all their equipment was unloaded and reassembled. By the time they were ready to be on their way again another day had passed.

"Say, younguns, road's not too bad today," said their father as they started out once more. "How'd you like to ride for a bit?" Franklin Graves was a good-natured man and let the younger children climb up into the crowded wagons from time to time. It was a treat to ride there, playing with the baby and trying to imagine what California would be like.

Their mother, Elizabeth Graves, was tall and thin, and her sunburnt face always wore a smile. She had many friends back home and soon made more among the families in the other wagons. The girls loved to go with her when she visited the women in the evening.

One night, Lovina and Ellen followed her over to one of the neighboring wagons to see how a young mother-to-be was feeling. Her baby was due any day now, and Mrs. Graves wanted to be sure everything was all right. Later that night they awoke to hear the young woman crying out.

"Baby's coming!" Sarah explained as she settled the youngest children. "Here, girls, take care of Elizabeth, and I'll go and see if I can help Mother."

It was a long night. When morning came, Mother and Sarah returned just in time to make breakfast. The look on their faces told everyone that the news wasn't good.

"We lost the baby," Mother explained. "And the mother isn't doing too well either. We'll have to help her husband out now while she gets her strength back." She shook her head. "This is no place to be birthin' children."

They made a bed in the back of the couple's wagon and tried to make the young wife comfortable, but without a doctor and proper medicine, there was little they could do.

The next day, the mother died too.

The men dug a grave and gently laid her and the baby to rest. Everyone was saddened by these first deaths on the long road west. Would there be others?

Within days, they reached the Missouri River, and again the wagons were taken apart, loaded and ferried to the other side. Lovina hadn't expected so much water again so soon. She began to wonder how they would manage the crossings later on when they were out in the wilderness. Would there be anyone to help them as they went farther west?

3

The Prairie

Independence, Missouri, was the last real town on the trail until Sutter's Fort in California. It was the "jumping-off place" for wagons headed west.

Lovina had never seen so many people in one place. Wagons, oxen, mules, horses, cattle, dogs, and people jammed the streets. Animal smells washed over her like a wave. "Whew! I thought walking along behind the oxen was bad, but this is terrible!" she said to Ellen, and covered her nose.

Hundreds of emigrants crowded into the hastily-built stores, paying outrageous prices for last-minute supplies.

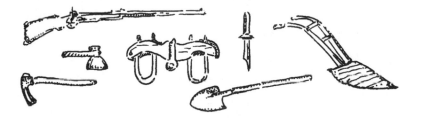

Most were buying grain and wagon parts. An extra axle or wagon spoke would certainly come in handy in case of a breakdown.

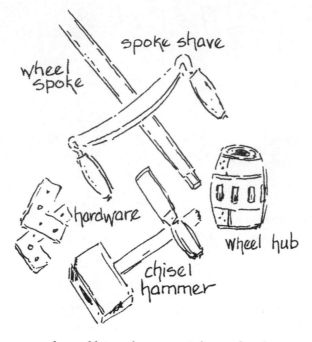

"Have you heard how the going's been for that train that left out'a here last week?" Father asked some men camped near them. He was anxious to hear the latest news and spent hours studying his maps and talking to anyone who might have new information.

After five days in Independence, he gathered his family together. "Well, folks, we'd best be on our way. The animals are rested and we've bought our supplies. Time to get moving."

Waving good-bye to friends, they started out into the unknown. They were among the last of more than two thousand travelers to cross the prairie in covered wagons that summer. Father estimated that it would take three or four months to reach civilization again.

The emigrants formed loosely-organized companies as they headed west. The Graves family traveled with first one group and then another. As the drivers walked beside the wagons calling out to the oxen, the cracking sounds of their long whips could be heard for miles around.

At night, the men took turns standing guard around the wagons and animals, in case of Indian attack. Whenever it was Jay's turn, Sarah stayed up to keep him company.

One moonless night when Will was on duty, he heard one of the men running toward him crying, "Fire! Indians! Fire!"

Will looked up and saw that the prairie was ablaze, but where were the Indians?

"Look, Will, look! See them over there, running towards us? There must be hundreds of them!"

Will stared in the direction the man was pointing, and then threw back his head and roared with laughter.

"Look again there, fool!" he cried. "Those aren't Indians. It's just those tall resin weeds blazing. I thought I saw some lightning a while back."

"By golly, you're right, Will. Don't you tell nobody now!"

"No, I won't," smiled Will. "Guess I'd'a been fooled myself."

And so the long days passed, walking, eating, sleeping, always out of doors. The girls wore sunbonnets tied loosely on their heads during the day to protect them from the hot prairie sun as they walked along, but after weeks of being in the sun, their fair-skinned hands and faces had tanned to a nut brown and the wagon tops were bleached to a stark white that shone against the sagebrush and grasses.

There were many jobs to keep them busy. Besides helping to prepare and clean up after meals, the girls were also expected to roast the coffee beans for breakfast, milk the cows, and help the younger children collect buffalo chips to burn for their fires.

"This is the job I hate the most," complained Ellen. "It was so much better when we had good pine wood to burn. These buffalo droppings still smell." On the plains, where there was no firewood, the dried droppings were all they had to keep their fires going.

In the morning, their father often placed a churn full of

sweet cream in the back of the wagon before they started. The jolting of the wagon churned it into butter by the end of the day. A bit of salt, and it was ready to eat with their supper.

Lovina often hummed *Home Sweet Home* as she worked. It made her sad to think she would never again see her friends, the familiar houses, churches and farms where she had grown up. She hoped California would be worth the hardships of this long journey. Looking out over the prairie, she made up her mind that no matter what happened, she would try to make the best of this new adventure.

They hadn't gone far when sickness hit the wagon train. Many people had terrible colds and dysentery, but the wagon drivers refused to stop when someone was ill. They had to keep going if they were to make it over the mountains before the winter snows. There was no time to waste. Those who couldn't walk were nursed in the back of wagons.

With so many falling ill, Lovina and Ellen stayed near their own wagons. So far, the Graves family had remained healthy, but they didn't want to take any chances.

As they traveled westward, the scenery stretching out ahead became more beautiful. One day the whole wagon train stopped at the top of a ridge to get a good look at the huge rock formations around them.

"This land is so big and wide. It feels like you can see forever!" Lovina said. "Seems like we should be able to see California from here."

"Now that would be somethin'!" laughed Will.

"Look over there, Will," Lovina cried, forgetting her sore muscles and blistered feet for a moment. "Doesn't that rock look like an old man with a pipe in his mouth? And that one, it looks like a big buffalo."

"You girls are getting silly," said their mother. "Why don't you take the young ones out to look for wild flowers?" The wagons moved so slowly the girls could walk out on the prairie for a short distance and not be left behind.

When they were making good time, the drivers stopped early in the afternoon to rest the oxen. Everyone enjoyed day's end when the wagons circled up to make camp. After grazing the animals, they herded them into the center of the circle of wagons to keep them from straying, and to guard them from rustlers.

Everyone had a job to do as camp was being made. "Over here, girls. We'll need more buffalo chips for the cooking fire. Take the young ones out to help you," Mother called. "Sarah and I will take care of dinner. Mary, you help your brother with the horses now, hear? There'll be time for visiting later."

Dinner was antelope stew that day. Mother and Sarah chopped and cooked all afternoon. This would be a special treat. Warm meals on the prairie weren't regular fare. There wasn't often time or supplies for such a feast. Usually their meal was beans and dried meat. After they had eaten, it was time for cleanup.

"Your turn to wash tonight, Vine," said Ellen. "I washed last night."

"Me again?" complained Lovina. "Why is it always my turn when there isn't any water around? Come on, Nancy, you're big enough to help."

"But I can't carry the bucket, Vine. It's too heavy!" whined Nancy.

"Now girls," scolded their mother, "that's enough complaining. You just get busy and get this job done. I think Jay's planning to play the fiddle for us tonight."

That was all they needed to hear! Soon everyone was hard at work.

Ellen and Lovina had to take care of the dishes each evening and pack them away for the next day. If there was a stream nearby, they would take a bucket and carry back water for washing up. But there was no water tonight. They would have to go out onto the prairie to find sand.

First Vine scraped off any leftover food. The scraps went to the dogs.

If there was water, her job was easy, but when there was none her work took more time. She would rub small handfuls of sand onto the plates and silverware, using a soft rag. Rubbing them slowly and painstakingly, Lovina gave them a soft shine. Wiping them clean again was the last step. That was Nancy's job. Keeping enough clean cloths for this was the hardest part. When they came to a stream, everything had to be washed and hung to dry. The older sisters sometimes helped, but they were usually kept busy with the younger children and the cooking.

"Time for a jig, girls?" Jay asked as he took down his

fiddle and began to tune it up.

The illnesses that had kept so many close to their own wagons recently seemed finally to have passed and everyone looked forward to an evening of fun.

The girls clapped their hands and hurried to find a place to sit as everyone gathered around the campfire near the wagons.

John Snyder, their driver, was the first to jump up and start the dancing. The younger girls were glad Father had asked him to come with them. But it was Mary who was the first to laugh at John's stories. Was this a budding new romance? Lovina hoped so. John's only fault was his quick temper when the animals wouldn't go where he wanted them to.

After the dancing, Jay played their favorite songs. Of course Lovina asked for *Home Sweet Home*. Everyone sang along by the light of the prairie moon. When the singing was over, Father told them stories about his adventures in Vermont, where he lived as a boy.

As the fires dwindled, the children were sent off to bed on their blankets under the wagons. The parents, tired after another long day, soon headed to their tents as well. If the evening was warm, they too stretched out under a wagon or beneath the cool night sky.

"See," Ellen said as they unrolled their blankets and got ready for bed. "I told you this would be fun, didn't I?"

Lovina felt a little foolish that she'd worried so much about making this journey. As she drifted off to sleep, she hummed her favorite song.

> Be it ever so humble,
> There's no place like home.

Now what were the next lines? Oh, yes...

> A charm from the skies
> Seems to hallow us there,
> Which, seek thro' the world
> Is ne'er met with elsewhere.

She hoped that wasn't true. Surely there would be another home for them somewhere out there.

When summer storms brought thunder and lightning, the sky would be as light as day one minute and as black as night the next. The loud claps of thunder frightened the girls. The sounds of oxen bellowing and children crying sent shivers down Lovina's spine. She lay awake, wet and cold in her blankets, listening to the howling wind and driving rain, wondering where the next day would take them. She was homesick for their warm house back in Illinois, with its dry, cozy beds.

It seemed that there was always something to worry about: rain, Indians, sickness, broken axles, lost children. But none of these worried Lovina half so much as the thought of the flooded rivers they'd heard were still ahead of them. How would they ever get across?

4

Big Water

Each day offered new challenges. After a heavy rain, the trail turned to mud and the wagons sank to their axles. Even unloading the heaviest boxes didn't lighten the load much, and the wagons were hard to pull. Some days the poor oxen couldn't move even the lightest wagons in the heavy muck and mire. All the travelers could do was sit and wait for the rain to stop.

One morning, on one of those forced stops, Lovina looked out over the prairie and saw, riding toward them, a group of twenty or more Indians. She drew back behind the wagons and began to tremble. Were these the "hostiles"

they had heard about?

Most of the emigrants had started across the plains thinking the land of the Indians was free for them to take. The natives had many reasons to resent these strangers: Food had become scarce, the emigrants were well-armed, and they didn't speak one another's languages. Neither group trusted the other. The natives wanted to put a stop to this migration.

The horsemen came to within a few hundred yards of the wagons and stopped. Finally, one tall Indian walked his horse to the head of the line. "Big water," was all he said and pointed to the west.

"No, no thanks, we're just fine," Father said, shaking his head.

The Indian shrugged as if to say, "Suit yourself," and as quietly as they had come, they headed off across the plains.

"I think he might be warning us that we'll need help crossing the Platte River up ahead," said Father to one of the other drivers. "These tribes will sometimes help get your wagons over the streams in trade for some goods."

"Oh I hope they don't come back!" Lovina worried.

Not long afterward, the wagons came to the rain-swollen river. The flood waters had spilled over the riverbanks, covering the land for miles around. Lovina was terrified.

How would they ever make it across all that water with no help?

Scouts set out to search for the best place to cross. They found several barges abandoned by earlier wagons and everyone went to work. One of the men swam his horse to the other side carrying a strong rope, which he tied to a tree on the opposite bank. This would become their guide as they ferried the wagons across.

As Lovina had feared, it wasn't long before the Indians reappeared, and this time a bargain was made. The natives agreed to help them cross the river, in trade for some of the women's jewelry.

Even with this help, the travelers had to lighten their load. As some of the men herded the animals into the water, others began to unload the wagons and lift the clumsy loads onto the awkward barges. The small wagons carried a lot of weight and it soon became obvious that it would be easier if they left some of the heavier items behind. Many other wagons had crossed here before them and they too had left treasures on the river bank.

"Just look at what people have thrown out, Vine!" exclaimed Ellen. They found rocking chairs, trunks of fancy clothes, tables, even a small pipe organ. "What a shame to leave all this behind."

With loud cursing from the men and muffled screams from the women and children, the oxen began pulling the awkward ferries to the other side. The rest of the frightened animals were driven across by the drivers, who fought to keep them headed in the right direction.

Lovina began to shake with fear. There was water everywhere she looked. How would they ever be able to get to the other side? She never dreamed when she left Marshall County that she would see rivers as wide as this.

When her turn came to cross, she slowly edged aboard and shut her eyes, her heart pounding wildly. She had never been so scared in her life. When the last wagon rolled safely onto shore, everyone sank to their knees.

"Lord be praised," said Mother. "I'm glad that's over."

"So am I, Mama, so am I!" Lovina was exhausted. She hoped they wouldn't soon have to face another of these rivers.

"Where's Will, Ellen?" Lovina asked one morning. "Father's been asking about him, and I haven't seen him anywhere around camp, have you?"

"No I haven't, Vine. Maybe he's gone off with the dogs to hunt."

"Father's not going to be happy about that. He makes such a fuss if any of us goes out alone. They need him to help with that cracked axle on Jay's wagon," Lovina said. "He'll be in trouble when he gets back."

Will had ridden out onto the plains and had spotted a large herd of antelope off in the distance. Enough meat for the whole train, he thought. He had soon gone farther than he realized. When he finally returned, his father was furious. "Where have you been, young man?" he demanded to know. "You know you shouldn't go wandering off like that! We haven't got time to be worrying about you with all the work to be done. Now tie that horse up and get busy!" he ordered and turned on his heel.

"But Father…" Will tried to answer. His father hadn't even waited for an explanation.

Not everyone on the trail that summer was going to California. Some were headed for Oregon, and planned to turn northwest on the Oregon Trail soon, leaving the Graves family with a much smaller company. They had been traveling with a large group of wagons from Kentucky for several weeks and had covered about thirty miles since they passed the south fork of the Platte River. Each night as they rounded up the cattle, they noticed that there were fewer than there had been the day before. Nearly a dozen were gone.

"We're going to make camp at Scott's Bluff tonight," said Father. "We need some time to work on the rigs, and we can have a look around to see if we can find some of the missing livestock. They've most likely been driven off by those Pawnee we saw hangin' around a few days back. Three of our best milk cows are gone, too," he told them as he and the other men saddled the horses and headed out to see what they could find. Will wanted to go with them, but his father told him he would have to stay behind to help his mother.

The women and children always worried when the men were away. Most of them could use a shotgun, but they would be no match for an Indian attack. Lovina's heart pounded with fear at the thought of a war party.

Late the next evening, the exhausted searchers returned to camp with bad news. The Pawnee had been lying in wait for them. Edward Trimble and another man had been killed. Poor Mrs. Trimble was devastated. She was pregnant with another child, and now, without her husband, she and the children's grandparents would have to travel on to Oregon alone.

The wagon masters gathered the remaining families together to discuss their plans.

"Gotta stay together, folks." said Franklin Graves. "It's too dangerous if we get separated. Now round up your cattle and let's be on our way." He would feel safer if they could find another party going to California.

As the days passed, Lovina began to notice that things were still not going well with Will and Father. Will was angry because his father had yelled at him, and because he was left out of the search party. He continued to complain about the tight rein his father held over his children. He wanted more freedom. The slow progress of the wagon train bored him.

"Really, Pa, I'm old enough to go on and scout what's up ahead by myself. There's plenty of tracks from other wagon trains to follow, and it'll help everyone in the train to know what's out there."

"No, Will, you're not going and that's that!" said Father. "There's too much work to be done with the wagons and the animals. I can't have you gallivanting all over the country. We don't need any scouts right now."

"Aw, Pa!" grumbled Will, and he stomped off.

One moonlit night, after several days of strained silence between the two, Lovina watched her father as he walked up the hill to where Will sat alone. The full moon looked near enough to touch and the bright moonlight shining down on the prairie gave everything an eerie glow. Lovina watched as Father lowered himself to the ground and sat beside his son. The two didn't speak, but sat silently looking out over the wagons circled below, listening to the sounds of coming night.

As Lovina got ready for bed, she could see the long shadows cast by her father and brother. "Dear Lord," she prayed, "please help them make peace with one another soon." She breathed as quietly as she could, hoping to hear their conversation.

"Evenin' son."

"Evenin' Pa."

"I've been wonderin', Will. Got any idea how long it's gonna take us to make Fort Laramie?"

It was the opening Will needed. He was pleased to have his father ask his opinion. Lovina watched as he straightened his shoulders. "Well, by my reckonin', it can't be too far ahead, Pa. We've been makin' pretty good time these last few days."

"I sure hope so," said his father. "Will you see what you can do about that noisy wheel tomorrow morning while we round up the cattle? I don't want to fall behind to fix it."

"Sure, Pa. I'll look at it first thing."

Lovina smiled as she fell asleep.

5

The Donner Party

As the wagons traveled westward across the plains, the Graves party sometimes met a scout or Indian trader bringing news. Several days after they left Scotts Bluff, they came upon a bearded old mountain man, who told them about a large group of emigrants headed by James Reed and the Donner families that he'd met several days ago. These emigrants had nine well-equipped wagons and were traveling with about thirty-one people from Springfield, Illinois.

"I'd say their train's about a week ahead of you folks," he told them. "The way I hear it, though, things haven't been going too well with this party, and they've been having quite a few arguments. I suspect several of the families may have left the main party already. Some were talking about going off toward the Fort Hall road.

"James Reed's been acting as leader of the wagon train, but I don't think that'll last long. He owns the best and fastest horses of anyone in the company, but a lot of those folks don't like his high and mighty ways.

"Besides that, Reed's got that big family wagon he had built back in Springfield. Claims it's the best-equipped wagon ever to cross the plains! You should see the things they've got with them. They have a library of books, a looking glass and even a cooking stove. They've even brought along a servant with them to help with the chores. I suppose some of the other folks are a little jealous."

"Maybe so," said Father. "Sounds like they've thought of everything though. What on earth's bringing them west?"

"Near as I can tell, Mr. Reed's run a successful business back East, but he feels there'll be an opportunity to make an even bigger fortune in the West. His wife, Margaret, has bad headaches, and they hope she'll do better in a milder climate.

"I don't know too much about the Donner brothers. Old George Donner's a sixty-two-year-old farmer. He lost his first two wives and married his current wife, Tamsen, about six years ago. They've had three children. Oldest one's only five. George and his brother Jacob decided they'd like a new start in California, too, I guess. Together, they've got about twelve children with them. They're both too old to be makin' such a move, if you ask me," the stranger went on.

Franklin Graves decided that for safety's sake, they should try to catch up with this bigger group of emigrants, not realizing that as the scout had predicted, the Reed/Donner party's leadership troubles had not ended.

Most of these men had not traveled in such mountains as these before. As the hills became steeper and harder to climb, the Reeds would not leave any of their personal belongings behind and the other drivers often had to "double-team" their heavy family wagon with their own animals. This slowed everyone's progress and added to their irritation.

Before long, people began to grumble. "We need to find us a new leader for this wagon train. Someone we can work with. Let's ask George Donner to be our captain."

And so mild-mannered George Donner was chosen to lead them. They would now be known as the "Donner Party."

Just a few years earlier, a young lawyer from Ohio, named Lansford Hastings, had led a wagon train west and what he saw there amazed him. There were forests of tall redwood trees, beautiful rolling hills and broad fertile valleys. He saw a land of opportunity in California, which was then the northernmost state in Mexico.

Hastings told his friends they should take California from Mexico and make it an independent republic. He would be its leader. He had even written a book called *The Emigrant's Guide to Oregon and California.*

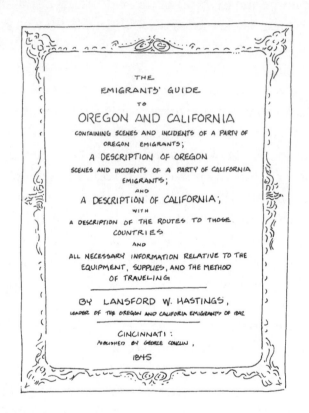

THE
EMIGRANTS' GUIDE
TO
OREGON AND CALIFORNIA
CONTAINING SCENES AND INCIDENTS OF A PARTY OF
OREGON EMIGRANTS;
A DESCRIPTION OF OREGON
SCENES AND INCIDENTS OF A PARTY OF CALIFORNIA
EMIGRANTS;
AND
A DESCRIPTION OF CALIFORNIA;
WITH
A DESCRIPTION OF THE ROUTES TO THOSE
COUNTRIES
AND
ALL NECESSARY INFORMATION RELATIVE TO THE
EQUIPMENT, SUPPLIES, AND THE METHOD
OF TRAVELING

BY LANSFORD W. HASTINGS,
LEADER OF THE OREGON AND CALIFORIA EMIGRANTS OF 1842

CINCINNATI :
PUBLISHED BY GEORGE CONCLIN ,
1845

Hastings suggested that any emigrants heading to California should take what he claimed was a new and shorter route across the great basin on the western side of the Wasatch mountains—south of the great salt lake instead of north. He assured them that it would take two hundred miles off the trip. What he didn't add was that he had only traveled the route on horseback, never with a wagon.

When the Donner Party reached Fort Laramie, they met a bearded old mountain man who had just ridden in on horseback. The old man told them he had been riding with Hastings. Now here was someone with real first-hand information!

Fort Laramie

The man's name was James Clyman, and he had been out to California to see for himself what this land fever was all about. James Reed and the Donners were eager to hear what he had to say.

Clyman had not been pleased with what he saw in California. He had met with greedy men and rough travel. When the Donners asked him about Hasting's cutoff, the old-timer shook his head sadly. "Don't try it! If you must go west, stay on the regular road. You'll never get your wagons across the Wasatch mountains and the salt desert if you take his route."

As usual, Reed took over. He listened to the old man, but refused to change direction.

"Now look here, men," he insisted, "I think Lansford Hastings knows what he's talking about. After all, hasn't he told everyone all about this new route in his book?

"And besides, doesn't luck seem to be with him? We've all heard about the wagon train he led safely to Oregon a few years back and the close calls they had with the Sioux along the way. It's a good thing to take your chances with someone who's lucky. Gamblers know that. And if you aren't something of a gambler, you don't have any business crossing the plains. People who aren't ready to take chances shouldn't be out here heading west!"

Now they must decide whether or not to heed Clyman's warning. If they followed the regular route to Independence Rock, over South Pass and the Little Sandy, they could then decide whether to take the new Greenwood Cutoff to Fort Hall or follow the old route to Fort Bridger. That would be

Fort Bridger

their last chance to change their plans. They would see for themselves what the mountain man had suggested.

When the Donner Party reached the fort, they found it was little more than a small camp run by two men named

Bridger and Vasquez, who provided supplies for the mountain men who came through hunting beaver. Bridger and Vasquez had recently hired Lansford Hastings to lead a group of wagons over his new route. Hastings had left word that he would come back to meet any other wagons who might still be coming through. Eager, ambitious pioneers like Reed and the Donners never questioned his plan.

"Now don't you folks worry. There's been lots of wagons passed by this way," encouraged Bridger and Vasquez. "You just go on and follow the tracks of them wagons up ahead. They're only a few days ahead a'you."

Of course these men urged the travelers to keep going. If Hasting's plan proved to be workable, it would bring more business their way.

What should the emigrants do?

After several heated arguments, more than half of the families decided not to take their chances on Hasting's route and turned north toward the old, well-traveled, Fort Hall road as the others had done, leaving only twenty wagons with the Donner Party. Half of the seventy-four people remaining with them were children.

6

Time of Decision

Meanwhile, the Graves wagons pushed forward. It was almost the end of June and they were nearing Fort Laramie. Most of the Indians they met were friendly, but word was out that the Sioux and the Snakes were warring with each other and that the emigrants should be careful.

One morning a group of fifty or more Indians rode up and began to circle the wagons, riding so close they could reach out and snatch small articles that were hanging from the sides. The emigrants never knew if the men wanted to trade or if they were looking for trouble. Lovina was terrified. When Father and the other men pulled out their rifles and began to wave them around, the Indians finally rode off.

Another afternoon, a band of Sioux joined the wagons and began bargaining with some of the emigrants. Mary and Will had been out riding and when they returned, one of the Indians wanted to trade for her, too. He seized the bridle of her horse as if to ride away with her. When Will realized what the Indian wanted, he raised his rifle.

That seemed to be warning enough. The Indians rode off laughing, leaving Mary shaking in her saddle. Though it wasn't funny at the time, everyone in the train teased her about her close encounter for a long time afterward.

It was the first of July. Lovina's birthday was only a few days off. She wondered if any of her family would remember. She didn't think so. There were so many children in the family that her parents were lucky to keep everybody fed, let alone remember their special days.

Lovina would be twelve this year, almost a grownup. Maybe some of the boys in the other wagons will be noticing me soon, she thought, like they have Mary and Ellen. But what on earth would she talk about with them?

She secretly watched Mary walking along with John Snyder. They seemed to have a lively conversation going. "Tell me, John," she heard Mary say, "how many buffalo do you think we saw yesterday?" What a stupid question, Lovina thought.

"Oh, I reckon there must'a been about a thousand!" John answered.

"Really?" answered Mary. Of course she knew how many as well as John did. Do you suppose she was just giving John a chance to show off a little bit, Lovina wondered?

Hmm! she thought to herself. Is that the secret? Do I just have to listen and play dumb? How silly! But Mary's announcement a few days later made the picture clear. She and John would marry when they reached California.

When the Graves wagons reached Fort Laramie on July third, they found that the Donner wagons had gone on.

As Lovina and Ellen straightened the bedrolls that morning, they noticed a wonderful smell. Was it?...no, it couldn't be, not here on the plains!

But just then she heard her mother's voice calling, "Get over here, birthday girl. Breakfast's waiting!"

"Happy birthday, Vine! Happy birthday!" everyone cried.

"Oh, Mama, flannel cakes, my favorite!"

Her mother smiled, "Well, of course, Vine. We couldn't forget your birthday now, could we?"

Everyone crowded around to have a taste of the freshly cooked pancakes that Mother had made.

"M-mm, that was delicious!" they all sighed. Meals like this were a rare treat. Breakfast was usually mush and coffee.

Father gave his daughter a squeeze as he walked past her.

"I promise you that next birthday we'll be in California, Vine."

Like Reed and the Donner brothers, Franklin Graves had heard the stories of Hastings' cutoff and the promise of this shorter and faster route interested him.

By this time, Hastings had left Fort Bridger, leading sixty wagons over his new route. He had left a message that any wagons who might still be headed that way should follow their tracks. He would come back to lead them through the mountain passes.

Like the Donners, Lovina's father was so eager to reach California he ignored all of the warning signs: no Hastings, no well-worn trail, no experienced leader to follow.

"It'll be fine," he assured his family. "We'll get there sooner this way." Lovina was still frightened after Mr. Trimble's death at the hands of the Pawnee, but her father insisted there was strength in numbers. They had to stick together.

Yet something didn't feel right to Lovina. "A lot of people have said this isn't the best way to go," she reminded Ellen.

Ellen put her arm around her. "We're all scared, Vine, but Father won't let anything happen to us. If we can just catch up with those other wagons, he's sure we'll be safe."

Leaving their companions who were headed to Oregon, they pushed on alone. When Ellen's birthday came just a few weeks after Lovina's, everyone wished her a happy day, but there was no special breakfast.

"I'm sorry, Ellen," whispered Mother as she tucked the girls in that night. "Things are just too uncertain right now. We'll have a big family birthday party for everyone when we get to California."

This was the part of the story that young Emmy never could figure out. Others had questioned this decision to take the short cut. She couldn't understand why her family had gone this way. Why hadn't they followed the California-Oregon Trail?

"Well, Emmy, as they say, hindsight is always better than foresight," said her grandmother. "I guess I was too young to understand at the time. But you know how people are; everyone likes to take a shortcut if they can. Someone has to be the first to try any new way.

"What none of us knew was that even though Hastings promised to guide any wagons coming behind him, he had no intention of coming back for us."

As the Graves wagons pushed on, the Donner party continued to work their way westward. The high flat plains between the ranges of the Rocky Mountains made traveling easier than they had expected. Only the high altitude slowed the animals.

By August 10th they had reached the rugged Wasatch range, and found that travel was much more difficult. In some places the track ran down narrow ravines and along dangerous hillsides that were barely passable. They found the Red Run Canyon with its colorful sandstone walls both beautiful and daunting. None of the travelers had ever seen anything like this country.

Beyond the canyon was a lovely mountain meadow, with plenty of grass and a clear stream. And after that, Weber Canyon.

"What's this?" A shout went up and everyone ran to see what the excitement was all about. There, stuck in the top of a bush beside the road, was a letter from Lansford Hastings.

James Reed picked it up and read, "The route below is very bad. I fear our party may not get through. Set up your camp and send a messenger to find us. I will guide you across the mountains by a better route."

James Reed chose two men to go with him, and the three set out. Eight days passed and they did not return. Their families began to worry. What could be taking them so long?

When Reed finally appeared back in camp his news was

grim. "We met up with Hastings near the foot of the mountains, but he wouldn't come back with us. He told us about another canyon over to the north, but the Weber Canyon here is practically impassable! The trail is so bad we barely got through. Our horses were half dead. Hastings had only this fresh one to spare. I had to leave our men at the other end with nothing to ride.

"I can't imagine how they ever got any wagons down there," said Reed. "The hillsides are so steep an ox can hardly stand up, and it's so narrow there isn't enough room for the wheels of the wagons alongside the river. There's thickets of trees everywhere, and in places there's huge boulders blocking the way. They've had to take their wagons apart and lift them up with ropes and winches to get them over. One day they lost a whole team over a cliff!

"We shouldn't even try to go down Weber Canyon," continued Reed. "Those folks had many more strong men with them than we do. We'd never make it through."

"Then what'll we do?" asked one of the men.

"Well, Mr. Hastings and I talked it over, and he suggested we go up over the top of the mountain. It's going to be rough, but we might have a better chance to get through."

With no other choice, they set off. It seemed doubtful that Hastings' route could have been worse. For the first three days they covered only a few miles. With such a small group, fewer than twenty axes were available for work, hacking and chopping their way through the thickets of aspen trees. These were not mountain men, and those who had hired on as drivers grumbled about the hard work.

7

The Meeting

On the fourth day, the workers heard some shouts coming from the hillside. What was this? Three more wagons were coming down the trail they had just made.

"What the…?" cried George Donner. "Hey there! What on earth are you folks doin' way out here?" Everyone stopped to see who these new people might be.

They were being joined by the caravan of Franklin Graves and his family: three wagons pulled by ox-teams, with drivers, women, a bunch of children, loose cattle, and barking dogs. The Graves family had finally caught up with the Donner Party.

The scene that met them was daunting, but it was obvious that the Donners had been hard at work. Piles of brush and trees lay all around and a makeshift roadway was leveled and shored up with the biggest logs.

Franklin Graves was first to speak. "Well, howdy, folks.

Looks like maybe you could use a hand here." Always the optimist, he chose to ignore the terrible condition of the road they had just come across and was smiling broadly as he walked forward and shook hands all around.

"Glad to see you, friend," said George Donner. "I'd say you couldn't have showed up at a better time. We've got a mighty big job ahead of us. Are these young men good workers?"

"Just you watch 'em," replied Mr. Graves, and soon the work was started again.

Lovina and Ellen were eager to meet their fellow travelers, but there was work for them, too. There was no time for socializing. From dawn to dusk, all hands were needed.

It took the girls days to sort out everyone in the Donner Party. So far they had met a large Irish family named Breen, the Murphys, McCutchens, some Germans, two Mexicans, and of course the Reed and Donner families. Lovina and Ellen saw that there were several girls who appeared to be about their ages. They smiled and waved as they went about their chores, but everyone was too busy to spend time getting acquainted.

With the newcomers adding thirteen more to their number, the Donner party now swelled to eighty-seven. More hands to do more work, and work they did! Long, back-breaking days of road building, carving a trail where no wagon had ever gone before. Everyone had work to do, helping with repairs, taking care of the animals and preparing meals. The girls helped carry logs and clear the thick, tangled underbrush. The men were needed to lift the wagons over the huge boulders in their path. By the end of the day, their hands were blistered and their shoulders ached from the heavy work they had done. Everyone was asleep before the sun set.

"Ellen, I didn't know there was so much hard work in all the world," said Lovina after another hard day of carrying brush out of the way of the new road. "I'm so sore I can hardly lift my arms, and just look at my shoes. They're worn through. I don't even have any blisters any more. They've all turned into calluses."

"I know, Vine. My hands look so bad, I think the only man who'll be interested in marrying me will be one of the mountain men. I look like an old lady! And it seems like we've hardly made any progress at all. I don't think we'll ever get out of these mountains."

Though over a week had passed since the Graves family had joined the Donner Party, the girls had still not had time to meet everyone. Lovina and Ellen continued to work together from dawn to dusk.

As she worked, Lovina thought of her song. "Do you remember that second part, Ellen?"

Lovina could remember snatches of the song…

> No more from that cottage
> Again will I roam.
> Be it ever so humble,
> There's no place like home.

…but no matter how she tried, she couldn't recall all of the verses.

When at last they reached the valley of the Utah River and came rolling down out of the mountains, everyone gave a sigh of relief. Here was fresh water, plentiful grass and finally the end of the mountains. Maybe now they would have time to rest and get to know the rest of the party.

But that was not to be. Not yet, anyway.

"We had better make up some of the time we've lost," Father told his family. It had taken them thirty days to cover forty miles. "We've got to keep moving or we'll never get to California before the snows set in."

The other wagon drivers agreed. They must press on. Coming at last out of the mountains and into the valley of the salt lake, the land began to get drier and water harder to find. A week after coming down from the mountains, they stood at the edge of the salt desert.

The wagons stopped, everyone in awe of the scene that stretched before them. Everywhere they looked there was nothing but white! There wasn't a tree or a blade of grass in sight, not a living thing anywhere. Off in the distance they could see several mountain ranges, but they were miles away.

Everyone walked slowly out onto the white stuff. They scuffed it with their shoes. It had a hard crust of salt. Finally someone bent over and tasted it. Sure enough, it was salt! They'd heard about it, but they hadn't believed it. And now here it was. There really was a desert made of salt!

"It's some thirty or forty miles to the other side," one of Hastings' notes had said. "You can easily carry enough water and grass for the animals, and water for yourselves. It should take about three days to cross."

But again Hastings had misled them. It was closer to eighty miles across! And it took them six sun-scorched days and bitter cold nights to travel over this stark white hell.

They weren't able to move more than a few yards at a time. By day, the heat was unbearable. Lovina's sunbonnet kept out the sun, but it only made her hotter, and there was nothing to quench her thirst. Her lips cracked painfully and bled when she opened her mouth.

The younger children cried for water, but there was none to spare. Though they tried to find shade near the wagons, there was no relief from the blazing sun. They were so thirsty they began to have visions of clear blue water on the salt beds ahead.

The nights were almost as bad, but it was the bitter cold that came to torment them now. They huddled together for warmth and pulled the dogs close to keep from freezing. The cattle lowed plaintively and sniffed the air as if searching for the scent of water.

"These poor animals will die if we don't get them to water," declared Father. He bathed the nostrils of his beasts with a wet rag and gave each one a swallow of water from his dwindling supply. If an animal wasn't pulling the wagons, it was turned out to fend for itself. Some died in their tracks, others wandered off into the salt desert and were never seen again. Seven of the Graves' cattle were lost.

One afternoon, Mrs. Donner brought out small pieces of sugar moistened with a few drops of peppermint and passed them out to the Reed and Donner children to help quench their thirst. The Graves children stood watching with dry mouths and parched throats, but they were not Donners or Reeds. It was not offered to them.

As the animals struggled to pull the heavy wagons, the drivers realized that the loads had to be lightened even more. They took out what wasn't absolutely necessary for their survival, to be left in the harsh desert. Some things were left

in shallow ditches, their owners hoping they would be able to come back for them someday. Four of the wagons were abandoned, their remaining supplies moved into the wagons of the others. The Reeds were forced to leave most of the treasures they had brought for their new life in California there on the desert. The big family wagon was all that was left.

These six days and nights took a terrible toll, not only on the animals and the supplies, but on the spirit of the emigrants as well.

"Whatever else happens, we must work together," said Father. "Time is our enemy now. Winter will soon be here. We've got to keep moving. We can't waste a single day." The Graves wagons were still intact, but many of their cattle were gone and their provisions were dangerously low.

When at last they reached the other side of the salt desert they found a few trees, some green grass and an open pool of water. George Donner called the families together.

"My friends," he began, "as you know, our situation is serious. We've taken some wrong turns and spent time we hadn't planned on. It looks like we won't have nearly enough food to last us at the rate we're going. The only way I can see for us to save ourselves will be for someone to go on ahead to get help and supplies."

Will Graves and Milt Elliott, one of James Reed's young drivers, were the first to volunteer. They had been out together looking for lost oxen after crossing the salt desert and had become friends. They felt they should be the ones to go. The wagon masters did not agree. "We're in strange country now, boys. We'd better send someone with more experience."

But who? None of the married men wanted to leave their families, and everyone was afraid that if they sent one of the single men, he might not come back. They were unsure of one another. Hardship had made enemies of many of them.

Finally two were selected. One was a tall man known as "Big Bill" McCutchen. He wept as he said goodbye to the wife and baby he had to leave behind. The other was a slender young bachelor named Charles Stanton.

Lovina and Ellen had noticed Charles looking longingly at their sister, Mary, in recent weeks, but Mary was "promised" to John Snyder.

Before the men left, Charles took Mary's hand. Looking deep into her eyes, he told her, "Don't you worry, Miss Graves, I'll be back with help just as soon as I can."

"We'll be counting the days, Charles. Good-bye, and good luck."

The two men were well-liked and trusted by the others. As they started off, everyone waved a sad good-by and the wagons continued their slow trek across the dry flat lands that lay ahead.

8

Paiutes

For a while their travel went smoothly after crossing the salt desert. The gently rolling landscape was easier for the animals to cover, and the sage brush and distant blue mountains were a pleasant change from the deadly white they had crossed. They followed Hastings' wagon tracks, making camp wherever he had stopped, but water was still scarce. Their half-starved animals were a sorry sight, and those mountains never seemed to get any closer. They were further away than they had appeared.

The wagons lumbered along for another three weeks, covering only a few miles each day. Everyone was tired and hungry, and as the days and nights began to get cooler, they could feel that winter was in the air.

"That time in the mountains and on the salt desert was some we could ill afford to waste," Father told them as they began another day. "If we don't find good water and food for these animals soon, they won't last much longer."

The wagon leaders finally decided it might help to divide themselves into two separate groups. Camping at different spots would give the animals a better chance to graze. The Donners and some of the families with faster rigs went on ahead. The Reeds, Graveses and the others followed behind. The problem now was that although this plan made each group smaller, they were not as safe.

Paiute tribes lived in this part of the country. Frequently the travelers saw the Indians in the distance, watching them or riding parallel to them, only to disappear suddenly.

Sarah knew that the children were worried too. She had become the unofficial storyteller for the young ones. One evening she called them together to tell them what she could about the Indians who lived around there.

"The Indians from around here are called 'Diggers,' because they use digging sticks to dig in the ground for roots or bulbs," she told them, "but they are not friendly to the emigrants. The wagon drivers have warned us to be careful. I think the Indians would like to trade with us, but we should stay close to the wagons just in case there's trouble. They really don't like us going through their lands."

Sarah was right. The natives were unhappy with these strangers crossing their country with their wagons and cattle. The emigrants overgrazed the meager grasslands, muddied the streams, and killed many of their people. It was not surprising that the two groups watched each other with distrust.

Late one afternoon in early August, just after they had set up camp in a small valley, several Indians suddenly appeared near the wagons. The girls moved closer to get a better look, when Lovina suddenly realized that the men had no clothes on.

"They're naked!" she whispered.

"Oh, my!" Ellen was surprised to see these men with only a loin cloth loosely covering their private parts. "Well I guess we must look pretty strange to them, too, with these long skirts on."

The Indians seemed friendly enough, smiling and nodding to the emigrants, but no one spoke the others' language, and it was hard to know why they had come. They apparently wanted to trade, but it was hard to guess what they were after.

"Get back over here!" ordered their mother, hurrying over to her daughters. "You stay by the wagons and watch the baby."

Only two of the Paiute men approached the wagons. The others stood back, watching quietly. They looked over the animals and indicated that they wanted to trade for one of the horses. The emigrants shook their heads, "No."

The two Indians returned to their friends but made no move to leave. What were they waiting for? When night came, the Paiutes moved out away from the wagons and set up their own camp not far away. Were they going to try to bargain for the horses again the next day?

But the next morning they were gone, along with a shirt and two oxen belonging to Lovina's father. Two nights later a horse was missing, again a Graves loss.

"Humph! They looked like they were gonna be friendly, but you can't trust 'em!" cursed Franklin Graves. There was nothing more he could do. They had to move on.

The wagon masters drove the animals as hard as they dared, but the pace was slow and labored. Patience and tempers were wearing thin. Petty arguments broke out. Crying babies and gossiping women made everyone tense. Fear was taking its toll on everyone.

Worst of all loomed the possibility of starvation. Families began to hoard their meager supplies.

"You younguns git on back to your own family now!" mothers scolded when children came near their wagons. "There's nothing here for you."

"Let me tell you, girls," said their mother after one of these outbursts. "Your father and I would never choose to travel with these folks if we had a choice, but a wagon's not safe traveling out here alone. We've got to keep together. Just stay close by. We'll manage somehow."

9

And On and On

As Lovina trudged along with this sad group, she began to lose hope of ever seeing California. They had long since passed the salt desert, but the land here was little better. Mile after mile, this dry expanse looked the same: sage brush, rocks and occasionally a little grass. Each day wore endlessly on to the next. There were no secrets, no laughter shared with Ellen any more. Only hunger and silent fear kept them going.

Though they searched the horizon every day for signs of McCutchen and Stanton, most of them believed they would never see the two men again.

"We've got to keep moving," encouraged Jacob Donner. "Snows will soon be here." He still hoped they could reach California before winter.

For weeks they continued through this barren land, along a small stream called the Humboldt River. In places it was scarcely more than a few stagnant pools, with bushes and scrubby willows lining its sides. River indeed!

Late one afternoon the wagons came to a steep hill.

"We'll have to double-team again, boys," yelled James Reed. John Snyder, driving one of the Graves wagons, tried to get past so he wouldn't have to wait behind the big Reed wagon. When one of his wheels became tangled with Reed's, his frustration boiled over.

Snyder yelled, "Git this damned wagon out of the way!"

"Now hold on there!" returned Reed.

"Move it!" yelled Snyder once more. The wheels would not come loose. Snyder's temper was out of control. He began to swing his long whip. More angry words flew. Snyder gave the whip another crack, this time hitting Reed on the forehead. Blood spurted from the wound. Again the whip lashed out, hitting Reed a second time.

Before anyone knew what was happening, Reed, in a burst of rage, jumped onto the Graves wagon, pulled out his knife and drove it into Snyder's chest.

"God, no!" cried Reed when he realized what he had done. "Help!" he screamed. "Somebody help me here!"

Will was walking behind the wagon and quickly ran to see what the commotion was all about. He was just in time to catch Snyder's body as it slipped to the ground.

"What have you done, you fool!" shouted Will.

Reed instantly regretted his action. He threw his knife into the river and ran back to John's side, but it was too late. Young John Snyder was dead.

Mary was hysterical. "John! Oh, John! Open your eyes! Speak to me!" she begged. But he was gone.

The others watched in disbelief. They had been through many trying times on this journey, with serious arguments and even some fights along the way, but no man had ever struck out at another in a way such as this. Had James Reed really meant to kill this man?

Reed offered some boards from his wagon to build a coffin for Snyder, but the others refused him. They built a rough box from parts of their own rigs and laid their young friend to rest.

John Snyder had been a very popular young man, a friend of Reed's they all thought. He was always full of fun and ready to lend a hand. James Reed on the other hand, with his proud ways, was not well-liked. Some wanted to hang him on the spot. What should they do?

Given the anger and frustration of the difficult journey, their decision at last was made. "Banish him!" they cried.

Lovina could hardly believe her ears! Even her father was calling for vengeance. She had liked John. He was like a brother to her. But she would never have chosen this harsh punishment for Mr. Reed. To send him alone into the mountains was a death sentence.

After Snyder was buried, James Reed said good-bye to his wife and family and rode off alone. Without a weapon, he would never make it. Perhaps the Donner brothers up ahead would help him.

Everyone was even more frightened after this. Things went from bad to worse. Trust was gone. Food and water were so scarce that no one dared leave any supplies unwatched. An old man named Hardcoop was put out and left to walk, or die, by the German family he had been riding with. They refused to carry him further.

"The oxen can't pull so much weight any more. We've got to lighten the load," was the driver's only excuse.

Only two in the party still had saddle horses, and they refused to go back for the old man. What good would it do to try? He was old and weak, and there wasn't enough food as it was. Mrs. Donner and a young father named William Eddy kept a fire burning all night for Hardcoop, but he didn't appear, and no one would loan them a horse to go after him. With heavy hearts they continued on with the others.

One of the wagons up ahead had done battle a few days ago with some Paiutes who tried to steal their horses. The Indians then lined up on the hills above the trail and began firing arrows into the frightened cattle. The emigrants were forced to finish off the poor wounded animals themselves. They cut off a few steaks to use before the meat spoiled, and left the rest behind. Between the desert and the Indians, nearly a hundred cattle had been lost. Lovina was frightened. How could they get by without these animals?

"'Scuse me, Mrs. Reed," said Milt Elliott, one of the drivers, late one afternoon. "I hate to be bringin' bad news, but these animals of yours just ain't gonna last much longer. This heavy load's more'n they can carry. If it was up to me, I think I'd unhitch the big wagon and load your things onto some of the smaller ones."

Mrs. Reed could see that the oxen were straining harder every day. "You're right, of course, Milt. Let's see what the others have to say."

And so the big Reed family wagon was abandoned. James Reed was gone, and Mrs. Reed and her children were at the mercy of the others.

"Guess you can use one of our wagons," said Lovina's father. "We've lost so many of our own supplies, there's room to spare now."

So the Reed's belongings were either stashed by the wayside or transferred to the Graves wagon. How sad to see the Reed's big family wagon left to decay by the side of the

trail! Though the two families traveled together now, it was in grim silence.

Every day they expected to find the body of James Reed by the wayside. When they finally caught up with the Donners, they learned that Reed had been joined by a man named Herron, one of Reed's teamsters, and the two had headed over the mountains together toward Sutter's Fort. The men had taken food for only a few days, planning to live off the game they could kill. Reed's family hoped that two men in the mountains would have a better chance than one traveling alone.

When the wagons finally came to the sparkling Truckee River, a great cry of joy went up. There was cool, clear, swift-running water, a meadow, and wild peas enough to pasture the half-starved animals. They could see the great Sierra Nevada mountains not far ahead. They had traveled over five hundred miles across scrubby sagebrush and at last they saw real trees. Maybe now they could rest.

But they must ford the river first. They had made twenty-one river crossings already on this trip, and each had been more difficult for Lovina than the one before. Instead of gathering more courage with experience, she seemed to feel it draining away. Lovina couldn't bear the thought of even one more!

She began to shake at the sight of the rushing stream. This late in the year the water wasn't as deep as some they'd crossed, but she had seen mountain streams before and knew they could be tricky. Maybe there would be deep holes! Would she be able to stand up?

"Oh please, Vine, don't be afraid. It's shallow. We can

wade across, see?" Ellen stepped out into the icy water, holding her skirts up above her knees. "Come on, it feels good!"

Lovina took a few tentative steps and found that she could indeed walk into the water without getting any deeper than her knees. Maybe this wasn't going to be so bad after all. "Br-r, it's cold, Ellen! Take my hand."

She reached out for Ellen to steady her, but before she had taken a step, she lost her footing on the slippery rocks and down she went.

"Help! I'm drowning! Help! Help!" Her screams could

be heard for the length of the entire train and brought everyone rushing to see what had happened. They couldn't help but laugh when they saw her sitting in the shallow water.

"Here now, Vine, stop your yelling! You're all right!" her father scolded, but he couldn't help smiling. He held out his hand and helped her back to dry land. "Keep your head about you, girl," he laughed.

"Oh, Father, I feel so foolish. I'm sorry I made such a fuss." Lovina buried her head on her father's shoulder.

"Well, you gave us a smile, Vine, and we could use that for sure."

"I wish this awful journey was over," Lovina cried.

"We all do, darlin'. It won't be long now."

Maybe their fortunes had finally changed. The desert was behind them and although they were far behind schedule, they could still get over the mountains before winter set it. It was only mid-October. The snows of the Sierra Nevada should hold off for at least another month.

A rest was certainly needed, but no one dared suggest that they spend much time here. They could spare only a few days. The wagons pulled to a stop and the animals were released to graze and drink. The travelers at last took time to refresh themselves.

The next afternoon a loud cry rang out, "Look! Look there!" At the top of the next hill stood Charles Stanton, along with two Indians and seven pack mules. Everyone rushed out to meet him, anxious to hear what he had to say.

"Tell us, man!" they cried. "What's up ahead? Will we be able to get through?"

"Yes, you will," he answered, "there's a little snow falling up there, but the pass is open."

"Thank God," sighed everyone in relief.

Stanton had seen Reed and Herron at the Johnson Ranch, not far from Sutter's Fort. He told them that the men were still alive, but so nearly starved he'd hardly recognized them. Poor Bill McCutchen had been too weak to make the trip back into the mountains, but Captain Sutter had sent along Luis and Salvador, two of his trusted Indian workers, to help bring the wagons over the pass.

"Now listen up folks," Stanton began, "and I'll tell what's up ahead. From here you'll travel uphill for the next day or two, but when you reach the summit you'll find an easy slope down into a small valley. Further on is some heavily forested country. About a quarter of a mile this side of Truckee Lake you'll see a small cabin, built by some folks who were caught by the winter snows a year or so ago. Just the other side of the lake is the pass.

"Now this'll be the hardest part. It's three or four miles straight up. There's a lot of boulders and only a few places to rest the animals, but once you get to the top it's not bad from there on out to Sutter's Fort."

Could it be? Were they really so near? Broad smiles covered the faces of these weary pioneers. They had travelled nearly 2,000 miles and there was only one mountain range between them and the golden land they had waited to long to see.

10

Snow So Soon?

Cheered by Stanton's arrival, they began to plan the next leg of their journey. First they would need rest and food. The animals were weak, but there was good grazing here. Even though they could see clouds gathering over the mountains, they decided to stop to rest before they made the next push.

After five days, the families whose animals seemed strongest started out again. Each family went on alone. Surely they didn't need to wait for anyone any longer. The Graves wagons were among the first to leave.

"Let's go!" called Mr. Graves excitedly, as they headed out of camp. "Once we get over that pass, we'll be on our way to Sutter's Fort." California at last!

Everyone was encouraged by the rest and a clearer picture of what lay ahead. One by one, the rest of the wagons headed onto the trail. On October 31st, they reached the lake and looked up to the pass beyond. They were a thousand feet below the mountain top, in a lovely valley with a beautiful lake. A great, high wall of granite boulders loomed above them.

One of the Donner's wagons broke an axle after several miles on the trail, and George Donner slashed his hand trying to fix it. The Donner families would not be able to join the others at the lake until Captain Donner's wound was tended. The rest of the wagons went on.

Some of the families began the climb toward the pass as soon as they reached the head of the valley, but Franklin

The pass at the head of Donner Lake

Graves decided to wait until the next day and get an early morning start. They made camp and spent a restless night. Tomorrow would be a big day.

But they had waited too long. Heavy storm clouds gathered, the sky became darker and the temperature started to drop. It started to snow before daylight. No one could travel in this storm.

As the snow deepened, the families who had tried to climb to the top were forced to return to the valley floor. They couldn't scale the slippery boulders and the trail was lost under a blanket of white.

The Breen family, who had been leading the wagons, were the first to spot the small cabin near the lake and hurried their six children inside.

The Graves family took refuge in their wagons. It continued to snow, and the temperature dropped even lower. They pulled their blankets and tarps around them and huddled together to keep warm.

The next morning, Lovina lifted the canvas covering their makeshift bed and cautiously peeked out. "Looks a little better today, Ellen. Maybe the storm's worn itself out."

"I hope so," Ellen replied. "Father will be anxious to get started."

Indeed, their father decided they should try to get over the pass as soon as possible.

Father and Will hitched up the wagon, and with everyone behind to help push, they headed toward the steep cliff. All day they struggled, the big animals pulling and straining against their harnesses, but they made little headway. The snow was too deep and the boulders too huge. Everyone was soon exhausted from the cold and the altitude.

"We'll have to abandon the wagons and go ahead on foot," Father ordered. "It won't be daylight much longer."

So, high in the mountains, far from civilization, they loaded the oxen with whatever they could and continued their climb, clambering over boulders as big as houses, carrying the youngest children, and coaxing the awkward animals onward. But the heavy oxen were worthless in the deep snow. These were not animals made to travel in the mountains, and they couldn't get a firm footing on the huge boulders.

"Looks like this is as far as we can go today," Father declared. "Daylight's giving out, but we must be nearly to the summit. We'll spend the night here and go on in the morning."

He found a pine log that was full of pitch, coaxed it into flame, and his exhausted family spent the night huddled around it.

"It's so cold," Lovina shivered. "I'm freezing!"

"Come close," said Mother. "If we all hold tight maybe we can keep warm." The children clung to each other all through the long night. When morning finally dawned, it was snowing again.

It snowed, and it snowed, and it snowed. It was all they could do to scramble back to the valley. For five days there was no letup. It was November 5th and they were trapped only fifty miles from Sutter's Fort and safety. They had lost their race by one day. If they had arrived at the lake just twenty-four hours sooner, they might have escaped ahead of the storm.

"Here, Will," called Father when they reached the valley floor. "Help your mother get the children settled. I'm going with the men make some shelter for us. We shouldn't have to camp here long, but we have to get out of this weather."

It was probably the worst winter of the 19th century. Emigrants had crossed the pass easily in December the year before, but the winter of 1846 was like no other. Never had anyone seen so much snow!

Meanwhile, James Reed had met Bill McCutchen at Sutter's Fort. Both were recovering from their near starvation in the mountains and had put on a few of the pounds they had lost. Their health had improved enough for the men to begin to make plans. It took several weeks before Reed and McCutchen were ready to go back into the mountains.

Once more Captain Sutter provided supplies: thirty horses, two mules loaded with jerked beef, beans and flour and two more natives to help drive the pack animals.

Of the original eighty-seven men, women and children who started out on Hastings' trail, only Reed's companion, Herron, was safe at last in California. Five were dead and seventy-nine were trapped in the mountains.

As before, they met with terrible weather. It rained steadily for days, turning the mountain streams into raging torrents. When they reached higher elevations the rain turned to snow. Their horses had to rear up on their hind legs and leap into the snow to make any headway at all. At times they would almost disappear in the heavy drifts. Further travel was impossible. They had to admit defeat and return to the fort. They must find more help and try a different route.

Captain Sutter felt the men could not get back to the rest of the party in the mountains until after the snow melted. None of them knew about the animals that had been killed by the Paiutes. Surely, Sutter felt, the stranded emigrants would have plenty of animals to kill for food. He encouraged Reed and McCutchen to take some extra time to stake their claims on some California land before they returned to their families. War was raging with the Mexicans in Monterey and most of the men at the fort had gone to help Captain Fremont in his fight to win California for the United States.

So Reed set off for San Jose, where he joined the California Battalion in the war against Mexico. He also made land claims for his family and others in his party. He arranged for the planting of a number of grape cuttings, some apple and pear trees and some barley.

It was the end of January before he began to search for volunteers to assist him in a rescue effort. Meanwhile, McCutchen was in Napa, also trying to get help for the entrapped pioneers. When all these people came together they were at last ready, but it took precious time to organize before they could head back. They had no idea how bad things had become.

Back at the lake, the emigrants were doing what they could to survive. Two more shelters had been erected and the families moved into these makeshift living quarters.

"There's water and wood nearby," said Father. "We'll just have to wait this bad spell out." No one guessed they would be here for four months. The roughly-made cabins had no windows and were roofed with only pine boughs, some canvas from the wagons, and hides of the oxen thrown over the tops. One cabin was about a hundred fifty yards from the original shelter that the Breens had found, and the other stood a good half-mile further downstream. This was

as close as any of them cared to be to the others. They had already traveled too long and too far together. Too many hard feelings had passed between them.

George Donner's family was about five miles back on the trail. They had put up three tents, which they covered with pine branches and quilts. George's hand still hadn't healed.

"We'll be a little longer," said Jacob Donner, when Franklin Graves rode back to see what was keeping them.

"George's hand is pretty badly infected."

The snow kept coming down and their simple shelters did little to protect them. Snow blew in whenever the tent flap was raised. As the temperature dropped their misery steadily increased. The men scoured the forest for firewood, but even when they found a fallen tree it was hard to keep the wet wood burning.

The cabins at the lake were arranged so that several families were housed together. Mrs. Reed, her children and servants, Stanton, and the two helpers, Luis and Salvador, shared a cabin with the Graves family, who had also taken in Mrs. McCutchen and her baby. Each cabin housed from five to eleven men, women and children.

"Poor Mrs. McCutchen," said Mrs. Graves. "She's had such a hard time tryin' to make do without her husband to take care of her and the little one. It's the least we can do. But goodness knows how we'll ever manage with all these people in here!"

The crowded cabin was divided in half by a tattered blanket hung from the ceiling. Each side cared for its own. Elizabeth Graves, like the other women, concealed her stores of food and took out only what she needed for each day's rations.

Even though their cabin was crowded, Lovina had never felt so lonely in her life. No one spoke for hours at a time and when they did it was with harsh undertones. "Gimme that!" or "You git outa here!"

The women hardly spoke to one another, except to bargain for someone else's meager supplies of beans or meat. They agreed to pay outrageous prices for what little they could wheedle from one another. Payment would be made when they reached safety. Even though they had plenty of cash, their money was of little use here in the wilderness.

"Are these the same people we started out with?" said Mother to Sarah one day. "We all had hope for a better life in California, but look at us now."

"I know," Sarah answered sadly. "I don't even want to think about it."

Lovina watched to see how the others spent their days. She often watched the Breens praying together and wondered if their Catholic faith was what gave them strength. They were the only family that seemed to accept the possibility that they might have to stay longer, and had begun to plan ways to stretch their food. They killed their animals as soon as they made camp, stored the meat in the snow outside their cabin and settled in for the winter. They ate the poorest meat first and measured out only what they absolutely needed for each day.

The other families were still hoping for a break in the weather and tried to keep their oxen alive to pull the wagons out over the pass as soon as it cleared. But they had no feed for the animals and were forced to let them loose to forage for themselves. Many of the big oxen became lost and died in the deep snow. Valuable food wasted!

"Mama," said Lovina one morning after they had been in the cabin for a week, "don't you think we should try to share what we have with the others? Maybe we'd be better off."

"Share with those greedy folks? It would never work. Can't nobody do more than we already are." Lovina knew better than to argue and turned sadly away.

She knew the women were mistrustful of one another and too frightened to admit they might not be rescued soon. Besides, if they killed their animals, how would they get their wagons out? How would she feed her own family, let alone the others, with supplies dwindling and no way of getting more?

Within a few short weeks there was almost nothing left except for a few odds and ends: coffee, tea and a little sugar. The remaining animals were their only hope, but so few could be found that the future looked grim.

As Lovina thought about their terrible plight, she wondered how they had come to this point? It didn't make sense. Her father had planned so carefully. He had lived in the mountains before, and they were sure they had brought plenty of food. They had travelled nearly two thousand miles and with so few to go, here they were at this dead end. Was it the shortcut or the weather that had betrayed them? What would become of them now?

Her only comfort came when she thought of her song. It rang in her ears:

> 'Mid pleasures and palaces,
> Though we may roam,
> Be it ever so humble…

She would give anything, anything, to see her humble home again.

"Oh, dear Lord," she prayed, "what's going to happen to us?"

By the end of November, they had slaughtered all of the cattle that could be found. Hunting and fishing seemed the only possibility for fresh food, but fishing for mountain trout demanded special skill and equipment, neither of which they had. Their hunting trips were not much more successful. A deer, a bear, an owl and a coyote were killed, but most of the animals had either gone down the mountains to warmer levels or were hibernating.

There were occasional sunny days between the storms, and on one bright morning, Will asked Lovina and Ellen to come with him out onto the frozen lake to see if they could catch some fish. Hungry as they were, they were willing to try anything, although none of them knew how to go about it.

Will pulled some string from an empty flour sack and made some hooks out of wire he'd found on one of the wagons. But what could they use as bait? Should they waste a piece of their precious meat?

They climbed out over the snow and slowly made their way onto the frozen lake. The sun shone warmly on their aching bodies, and their hearts were full of hope. How

delicious a taste of fresh fish would be to their starving family!

Will began to chip away at the ice until he made a hole about the size of a small round bucket. As Lovina stared down into the icy water below, her body began to quiver. "What is it, Vine?" asked Ellen. "You're shaking like a leaf."

"The water!" Lovina cried. "The water! I can't swim! We'll drown!"

"Stop it!" demanded Will. "Nobody's going to drown! For goodness sake girl, this hole isn't big enough for you to fall through even if you tried. Now pull yourself together. I need your help here!"

Ellen and Will helped her sit down on the ice. Her heart raced, but she tried to get control of herself. She looked around at the mountains. They really were beautiful. She sat very still, and soon began to feel somewhat better. She was even able to hold onto one of the fishing lines they had made.

"Look," Will whispered excitedly. "I can see four or five big ones down there! Come on, fishes, come to dinner."

But try as they might, they had no luck. The fish swimming around their hooks seemed to be slightly curious, but they didn't even nibble the bait. Ox meat was evidently not part of their diet.

After an hour of sitting on the freezing ice, the fishermen had to admit defeat, and glumly they made their way back to the cabin. Another day of hunger.

They tried to catch fish several more times over the next few days, but without luck. Starvation seemed even more real.

11

The Snowshoe Party

Things had gone from bad to worse. Their food was gone, and the snow continued to fall. They wouldn't survive if they didn't get help.

It was near dusk on the evening of December 6th when Franklin Graves gathered his family together to make an announcement. "Some of us have decided to go for help. Anyone who feels strong enough will be welcome to come with us. The rest will have to wait here. It's the only way."

Lovina and Ellen were among the first to volunteer, but Father insisted that they stay behind to help their mother.

By the next afternoon they had a group of fifteen willing to try an escape over the pass. There were nine men, five women and a young boy. Charles Stanton, Lovina's father, Mary, Sarah, her husband Jay, Amanda McCutchen and William Eddy were among the volunteers. Mrs. McCutchen would leave her baby behind for Mrs. Graves to care for. Even if they failed, there would at least be fewer mouths to feed back at camp. They called themselves, "The Forlorn Hope."

Franklin Graves had grown up in Vermont and had a little more experience with heavy snow than the others. He showed them how to use strips of leather and wood from the oxbows to make crude snowshoes. The shoes kept their feet from sinking into the deep snow, but the shoes were awkward and in their weakened condition, travel was painfully slow.

"Take care of your mother and the little ones," Father told his children before they left. "I promise we'll be back with help as soon as we can."

Though her father's words were brave, Lovina could hear the worry in his voice. She wondered if they would ever see him again.

On December 16th, the snowshoe party set out for Sutter's Fort, knowing deep inside that it would take a miracle to get them through. Lovina, her mother and the other children watched this pitiful group, struggling up the mountainside, until they were out of sight.

Stanton, with his experience in the mountains, was the leader. Each person took only six days' provisions. One day's food consisted of a strip of stringy dried meat, a little coffee and some loaf sugar.

For two days they struggled up the cliff to the pass at the head of the valley, then slowly continued their painful journey westward, their starved bodies exhausted by the tremendous effort and their eyes blinded by the bright sun that shone cruelly on the white snow.

Stanton walked beside Mary for a time, but he soon fell behind. He had been on starvation rations for so long that after the sixth day, he began to falter.

"Aren't you coming?" asked Mary.

"Yes, I'll be along soon," he answered. But this brave little man, who had already made the journey all the way out to Sutter's Fort and back again, could go no further. He had done his best to save his friends, but fatigue, snow-blindness and starvation had taken their toll. He was so weak he could go no farther. As he lay down in the snow, he closed his eyes and was gone.

"No, no!" Mary cried. "What will we do now?"

"Poor fellow," her father replied, "he did his best, but these mountains were too much for him! We've got to keep going, Mary, be strong, be strong." They buried him as best they could in the deep snow and sadly continued on.

Without Stanton's leadership, they were in trouble. Luis and Salvador, the Indians Sutter had sent back with Stanton, led them on what they thought was the trail they had traveled earlier, but they became confused in the snow and the group was soon lost.

Back at the lake, the cabins were buried under five feet of snow. Their only access to the outside was up some steps Franklin Graves had carved into the snow bank.

Lovina knew there was little chance anyone would get back to them soon. She and Ellen were determined to do what they could to cheer the younger children. They made up stories, played games, sang songs and took turns reading the few books they had saved. Again and again they read *The Life of Daniel Boone* and stories from the *Bible*, but the starving children were too ill to pay much attention and slept most of the time.

Everyone suffered from terrible pounding headaches. Lovina's eyes hurt so badly she couldn't bear to look out at the whiteness of the snow, and she thought she was seeing things that she knew weren't really there. One day she could have sworn she saw oxen dancing on the frozen lake.

When Christmas came, Mrs. Graves fixed them a special treat, beans and tripe, the first real meal they had eaten in weeks.

Lovina had been tucking away small bits of her own food each day. She wanted to be able to offer an extra nibble to one of the younger ones when she saw how hungry they were. Trying to distract the children from their hunger pangs helped to keep her mind off her own troubles.

By the end of December their food was completely gone. They had killed the last of the oxen long ago and now the ox hides overhead became their main food source. They mixed pieces with bark and melted snow, and cooked it until it thickened into a slimy gray glue. They tried to eat this sickening mess, but even though they were starving,

many gave up and ate nothing.

As the last of the hides were removed, snow came falling in and parts of the cabins were left open to the weather. The thin branches that were left couldn't keep out the snow and the cold. Most of the people spent more and more time in bed, wrapped in blankets and quilts, or huddled together. Several of the mothers still had nursing babies. They pleaded for scraps of food to keep themselves and their babies alive, but there was nothing for them. The smell of death hung in the air.

Lovina was glad that Will had stayed back with them. But even with his help, they were in great trouble. The fires had to be kept burning to boil the hides and bones to keep themselves alive, but wood was hard to find and cut, and it was all Will could do to keep them supplied with fuel. Though he wasn't much older than she was, just having him there made her feel that Father's spirit was somehow present.

Even the hides were nearly gone now. Faces were gaunt with hunger, loose skin hung from their bodies, and their voices were so weak they could scarcely be heard. Babies didn't even cry. How long could they all hold on?

The old and weak were first to die. In their starved condition, it was all their families could do to drag the bodies out onto the snow for a simple burial.

Between storms the days were sometimes clear and sunny. As Lovina climbed up out of this poor shelter one morning for a breath of fresh air, the scene that greeted her nearly took her breath away. The blanket of clean, new snow had taken on a gleaming whiteness that made the mountains look like a shining castle in the distance. How could nature be so cruel?

Father and the others were still out on the trail. She wondered if they had made it to Sutter's Fort. Would they find anyone to come back for them? Would anyone still be alive when help came? She was so tired and weak she hardly cared any more.

12

Starvation and Death

Meanwhile, the Snowshoe Party was struggling vainly through the deep mountain snow, growing weaker every day, with no sign of help in sight. Their meager provisions had run out and they were completely without food. Several lay dying in the snow.

Franklin Graves and Jay had both begun to stumble and fall. "You've got to go on without us, girls," Father told Sarah and Mary. "You must get help to the others!"

"No, no, we can't leave you!" they cried, "We need you with us! Who will show us the way?" But despite their tears, their father closed his eyes and was dead. Within two days, Jay was gone too.

Sarah and Mary began to panic. Without their father and Jay, how could they go on? They were sure that they too would soon die. But somehow, the will to live and the knowledge that their families were depending on them gave them the strength to carry on. Their party had dwindled to a

The Route of the Donner Party

handful, but somehow they kept going.

They made slow, painful headway for several days and at last, when they thought they too must give up, their fortunes finally changed. Several Miwok Indians, out on a hunting party, found this sad group sitting together near some trees, staring absently into the woods, feet bleeding, too weak and dizzy to even notice the deer who wandered close by. The Indians offered them ground acorn bread, seed and water, but few of the emigrants could keep the food down. They had been starved for so long. Their stomachs could hold only the water and soft green grasses.

The first white settlement on the western slope of the Sierra Nevada mountain range was Johnson's Ranch. The

Richie family had barely escaped the heavy snows of the recent winter and had decided to spend the winter there.

"What's this!" cried Mr. Richie when the Miwok arrived at the ranch, carrying William Eddy. Eddy was barely able to communicate with them.

"Bread!" was his first word.

And then, "Others out there. Need help!"

Mr. Richie rounded up his horse and two mules. Mrs. Richie gathered some bread, a few dried apples and some blankets, and Mr. Richie hurried out to look for the rest of the party. It had been thirty-three days since this sad group left the lake, with only a six-day supply of food. Only seven of the fifteen had made it through—all five of the women, only two of the men.

The women had been the strongest. Sarah and Mary, along with Sarah Foster, Harriet Pike and Amanda McCutchen, all lived to see California. Only William Foster and William Eddy of the ten men survived. When they were brought in to Johnson's Ranch, they were so near death they would not likely have made it through another day.

The Richies gave them food and a place to rest. As soon as they were able to travel, they continued on to Sutter's Fort to plead for help for their families left back in the snow.

When he heard the story, Captain Kern, the commanding officer at the fort, offered three dollars a day to anyone who would volunteer to go into the mountains to rescue the stranded emigrants. But who would be foolish enough to try?

At last, seven agreed to go. Although they knew it would be dangerous, these were men whose hearts could not let them look the other way when their fellow man was in trouble. They were led by a tall, slender man named Reason Tucker, who knew the Donner party well. He had traveled with them earlier on the trip, but had been with the group who decided against taking Hastings' cutoff, and had come by way of the Fort Hall road. Tucker's family had made it over the pass just before the winter storms.

On January 31st, this brave group of men was ready to start back into the mountains, driving pack animals loaded with food and provisions. None of them was a mountain man, two were sailors and several were emigrants themselves. No one from the Snowshoe Party was strong enough to go back with them.

Travel was still difficult. The deep snow made the passes hard to find. But the rescue party hurried on. Two more weeks had gone by and they knew that without their help these people would have no chance.

When the men finally reached the highest pass and looked down into the valley below, they saw nothing...nothing but snow! No traces of life. It was February 18th, sixty-one days since the Snowshoe Party had set out in search of help.

Had they arrived too late?

13

Help At Last

They called out a tentative, "Halloo there!" No answer. "Anyone here?" Was there no one left alive? At last a woman appeared, poking her head up like an animal from a hole in the snow.

Dizzy from the cold and weak from hunger, she cried, "Are...are you men from California, or do you come from heaven?" As others began to crawl from the cabins, they wept, "Relief! Thank God, relief!"

Lovina and Ellen were in the woods searching for pine cones when they heard the shouting. They had all but given up hope of being saved and thought at first that they were hallucinating again, but the voices called once more. Could it really be help at last? They could hardly believe their ears, as they hurried back to the cabins.

"Help at last! Where are Father and the others?" they cried.

"Later, girls," was the only answer the men would give.

Reason Tucker and his men knew the dreadful story of the Snowshoe Party could wait. They dared not discourage the already disheartened families here in this mountain prison. There would be time enough to tell them the story when they reached safety.

Many of the emigrants were nearly dead from starvation and exposure. Because the stomachs of these starved people could handle no more than a few mouthfuls at a time, the rescuers were careful about how much food they gave the survivors at first. Mr. Tucker stood guard and saw that none of their precious food was wasted. After everyone was fed, he posted a guard and finally the exhausted rescue party was able to sleep.

After the men had rested for a few hours, they began to take stock of what they faced. Twelve were already dead from starvation and it was clear that time was running out for many others. Of the forty-eight still alive, some were beyond help. A few of them had gone mad.

"Looks like we won't be able to take everybody with us this first trip out," said Mr. Tucker. "We'll take the children and a few of the women first, but they've got to be able to walk on their own. Mrs. Reed, you and your children and these bigger Graves kids look like they'll be able to travel, and we can take that young Donner boy. All right with you?"

"Of course," replied Mrs. Reed.

So Tucker and his men selected twenty of the older children, including Lovina, Ellen and Will. Mrs. Reed with her children and the other youngsters who appeared strong enough would join the group as well.

The rest would be left at the lake to await the next rescue party. Mrs. Graves with her baby and the three younger children must stay behind. The rescue team had not brought enough food for everyone. They would need supplies for themselves and those they were leading out. There was almost nothing extra for those left behind. Things would be as bad as before.

When the time came to depart, Lovina and Ellen wept uncontrollably—for their mother, the young ones, and the uncertainty of what lay ahead. Lovina would never forget the look on her mother's sweet face, so drawn and pale as she gathered her children close beside her. She held a handful of coins in her hand.

"I have eight hundred dollars here, children. It's all the money we have in the world. Your father had it hidden in the wagon bed, stacked in holes that he drilled before we left Illinois.

"I've decided to hide the money again right here until your father comes back for us, but you may need to buy something for yourselves when you get to Sutter's Fort."

She carefully opened the bag. From it she took five coins and handed one to each of them.

"These are for Sarah and for Mary, Will. You must promise to come back for the rest if I don't make it out. And you take good care of each other now, hear?"

She smiled bravely at her children.

"Don't you worry, Mama. We'll be all right," said Will. "And you will, too. That money will be safe. I promise to see to that. We'll be together before you know it."

The hardest thing Lovina would ever do in her life was to say good-bye to her mother and the children they'd leave behind. She knew it might be the last time she would ever see them. She tied her coin in the corner of a piece of cloth and stuffed it deep into her pocket to keep it safe. Ellen did the same. Will put his own coin and the two for Sarah and Mary into his leather coin pouch.

Lovina had nothing but the few tattered rags she wore on her back. She wrapped an old shawl around herself and tried to imagine what it would be like to finally be out of this terrible place. Try as she might, she couldn't picture anything but snow.

"Well, we're ready to go," called Mr. Tucker. As they joined the others gathered on the valley floor, Lovina, Ellen and Will waved a last goodbye and began the slow climb to the pass, inching their way over the snow and rocks in their final attempt to reach the safety of the valleys lying to the west.

Travel in the rugged Sierra Nevada mountains was hard, even for the strong and healthy in good weather. Yet here was this pitiful group of frail children with no heavy shoes, warm clothing or enough food to give them the extra energy they would need, trying to claw their way over the snow-covered granite boulders and into deep ravines that covered these mountains. They fell often, but not one cried out. They understood that they had to be strong, to take care of themselves. Would they win this race with time? Would the mountains again take their toll?

Not all would escape alive. One died soon after they left the lake, and had to be buried in the snow. It was soon apparent that two of the smaller Reed children were too weak to keep up with the others, so one of the guides took them back to the valley and left them with the Breen family.

Not long after that, one of the men in the rescue team found that he too was so weakened from cold, hunger and exhaustion that he could go no further. "Please," he begged, "just leave me here! You must get the children out!" There was neither time nor energy to argue. They must keep going. They left him by the side of the trail.

Mr. Tucker's group had left the cabins on Monday. By Friday afternoon they were within a day's journey of Bear Valley. They had been moving at such a slow pace that the men began to carry the weakest children who were last in line up to the front and then return to pick up the next slowest, making a steady relay down the hills.

As Mr. Tucker lifted some of the children, he was shocked to see that they had been chewing on strips of his leather pants that had torn loose.

Early on Saturday morning, they caught sight of some men moving through the trees ahead. It was James Reed and Bill McCutchen, returning with another rescue party. Reed's family was overjoyed to see him again, but he couldn't stay. He must collect his two young ones back at camp.

They parted once more. After Reed reached the valley and located his own children, he went on in search of the Donner families. He found that Jacob Donner and his wife Elizabeth had both died. George Donner lay dying from his badly infected wound. There was no way to help him. His wife, Tamsen, refused to leave her husband, so Reed was forced to leave his old friends on their own.

Reason Tucker and his sad little group continued down the mountain. Their future looked brighter when they located some food they had hidden in Bear Valley on their way in. But they hadn't foreseen the reckless despair of these hunger-crazed youngsters. Jacob Donner's young teenage stepson waited until everyone was asleep that night and sneaked back to the food supply, where he greedily gorged himself. It was more than his weakened body could digest. When they found him the next morning, he was dying. He lasted only a few hours. They buried the boy in the snow and continued on.

Within days, they met another rescue team bringing more food and this time, extra horses. As the men helped the exhausted Graves girls up into the saddles, Lovina's eyes filled with tears.

"We're going to make it, Ellen," she softly cried, "we're really going to make it."

As they worked their way out of the mountains, down into the foothills, they came to the last patches of snow. This awful winter was nearly over.

Once into the foothills, the season changed quickly from winter to spring. The sun shone warmly and the road wound through pines and chaparral. There were birds and small animals everywhere. This pleasant scene seemed like a dream to Lovina. Could the nightmare really be over?

14

Sutter's Fort

By the time they reached Sutter's Fort, it was almost the end of March. Nearly six months of their lives had been spent trapped in the mountains.

News of their arrival spread quickly among the settlers. Everyone rushed out to meet them as they came into sight. Lovina was moved to tears as people reached for her hand, as though just by touching her they could offer help.

Sarah and Mary were first to greet them.

"Oh, my darlings," said Sarah, tears streaming, "you're finally here! Is everyone all right?"

"Yes, yes, tell us!" cried Mary. "Where is Mother? And where are Nancy, Jonathan and Franklin? Who has the baby?" Everyone seemed to be asking questions at once.

"We…we don't know where they are!" It had been nearly two weeks since Lovina and Ellen had seen their mother and the young ones.

"Where are Father and Jay?" they asked.

"They didn't make it," Sarah sadly told them. "They did their best, but without food they just couldn't go on."

"Dead? Oh, no…not Father, not Jay! That just can't be! What will happen to us now?" Lovina was heartsick. She wanted to cry, but she was so completely exhausted her tears wouldn't come. When they finally did, she thought they would never stop.

Emmy stopped her grandmother again. She was curious about those stories of how the Donner Party had cannibalized the bodies of those who had died. "Grandma, did that really happen?"

"Yes, dear, I'm afraid it did, Not until their situation had become desperate, however, and not until after Ellen and I had been rescued. But I have spoken to some of the others, and I think I understand now how that must have happened.

"These people were nearly dead from starvation. They were desperate for anything that might keep them alive. They boiled and ate hides, grass, insects and bark…and when that was all gone, they looked around…and there were the bodies. It seemed like a reasonable choice. There wasn't much left of their poor dead comrades; most were so thin there was little but skin and bones, but maybe…maybe if they pretended it was a deer or a squirrel someone had killed, maybe the little flesh left would keep them alive just a few days more.

"Starvation is a terrible way to die, Emmy. People change. The pain is so unbearable they're no longer in their right minds. Starving is the only thing they can think about. Starvation is like a wolf stalking its prey, and you must outwit the enemy!

"It's hard to imagine these horrible times. These poor people were haunted with the memories of what happened to them for the rest of their lives..."

Sutter's Fort
Established as a fort in 1839 by John Sutter, it became an important trading post and place of refuge in early California.

Settlers at the fort took the Graves girls into their homes to await news of the rest of their family. Lovina's poor body longed for sleep, but even when she drifted off, her rest was fitful. How could she sleep after all she had seen? Her dreams were filled with the terrors of the past months, and now with her father gone, she couldn't begin to guess what their future might hold.

When James Reed and Bill McCutchen brought out the next group of survivors a week later, their mother was not with them, nor were the three youngest children.

More terrible news! Their mother and Franklin had also died in the cold mountains. Jonathan and baby Elizabeth were taken to Johnson's ranch, but they too had perished. They just weren't strong enough to withstand the months of cold and starvation. Only nine-year-old Nancy had survived and made it out to Sutter's Fort. They found her in back of one of the wagons, weak and thin, but alive!

The poor child was in no condition to tell them what she had seen. "M-Mother's gone!" she sobbed.

The girls were grief-stricken! How could they have lost so many? Half their family was dead—what a terrible price to pay! Was California really worth all this suffering?

"What will become of us now?"

Sarah was now the head of their family. She gathered everyone close around her in a quiet, shaded spot just outside the walls of the fort.

"I know it seems like we've come to the end of the world," she began, "but we've got to be strong! We just can't give up now. We've got to remember why we came here. Father wanted a better life for all of us, and he knew that this was the place where opportunities would be found.

"Maybe we've survived these terrible times because we have important things to do with our lives. We must keep going; we've already come too far to give up. It's 1847, we're alive, and we're in California! It's up to us to make Father's dream come true.

"I've been talking with some of the settlers. Several families have offered to help us. Mary, Will, Ellen and I are old enough to take care of ourselves, but I think it's best if Lovina and Nancy stay with some of these kind folks for a little while. We'll send for you as soon as we get settled."

"Go off alone?" Lovina worried. "How can I go off with strangers all by myself?

"Why can't I go with you, Sarah? Please?"

"No, Vine," answered her sister. "I can't take you with me. I'm not even sure where I'll be living for a while. You must be brave, Lovina. You and Nancy won't be far from each other and I promise we'll be together before too long."

What other choice did they have?...

The next morning Will took Lovina outside.

"I need to talk to you, Vine," he said, taking her hand. "I've decided to go back into the mountains again. I know I probably won't find anyone alive, but I'm going to look for that bag of coins Mother had with her. She made us promise to come for it if she didn't get out."

"But, Will," Lovina cried, "it's too dangerous for you to go back. Please, don't go!"

"Now, Vine, don't you worry, I can take care of myself. I've talked to some of the other emigrants, to see if anyone knew anything about some money she had. Some claim it never existed, but we've seen it ourselves. It's got to be there somewhere," Will went on.

"And I've met someone who was with one of the rescue parties. He told me he'd seen Mother back there—said she was pretty bad off. He thought she was raving mad when she began telling him about the money. She told him she was afraid James Reed was going to come and steal the coins from her and that she was going to bury them. He thought she was out of her head, so he didn't pay much attention to her.

"See, Vine," said Will, "I have something to go on now. If I can't get Mother out alive, at least I can do that much. I'm going to find those coins, you'll see!"

Lovina wondered if she would ever see her brother again. Would she go back into the mountains? Never!

15

1847 – Pueblo San José

When the settlers in Sutter's Fort heard the details of the Donner tragedy, their hearts went out to the survivors. They knew these stories could as easily have been their own. They offered homes to the younger orphaned children. The older ones were taken in by families who could use an extra hand.

Isaac Branham and his wife were among these early pioneers. They had been visiting relatives at Sutter's Fort when the rescue parties returned and were among the first to offer help.

"Lovina, dear," said Mrs. Branham, after they had come to know the Graves children, "Isaac and I would like you to stay with us at the ranch for a while, if you'd like. At least until your sisters get settled. We're near Pueblo San José, about a day's ride south of San Francisco Bay. We have plenty of room, and I understand Nancy will be with some relatives of the Donners, not far from us. You could visit each other whenever you like. Would you like that?"

"Why thank you, Mrs. Branham. That's very kind of you." Lovina knew she was lucky to have met this generous family, but she hoped she would be able to join her older sisters soon.

The older girls would not be far. Ellen was to move north to Sonoma, and Sarah to the Napa Valley. Mary was going south to San Luis Obispo. Will, of course, was headed back into the mountains.

Lovina turned from one to the other of her family as they said their good-byes.

"You'll write to me now, won't you?" she pleaded.

"Of course," promised Sarah and Ellen. "And we'll send for you just as soon as we get settled."

After so long in the cold, deep snow of the mountains, Lovina loved the sun-baked warmth of the wide sweeping valleys they crossed on their way west. How her parents would have loved this country! She wondered if the California sun always shone so warmly. She felt calm for the first time in months as she rode along in the Branham wagon, under the clear blue sky. A heavy load seemed to have lifted from her shoulders.

When they reached the pueblo at San José a few days later, she was curious when she saw the thick-walled adobe buildings, and the workers tending the orchards and gardens. The men and women working in the fields were brown-skinned, but were not dressed like the natives they had met on the trail. These people were dressed more modestly in woven shirts and long skirts, and many wore their hair in braids. They waved as the family drove past. How different from those she'd met on the plains!

The days passed pleasantly as Lovina settled into the easy life at the pueblo. The Branhams did their best to help her adjust, but grief often overtook her when she least expected it, and she spent many hours in her room, thinking about her family, alone with the misery of the past months.

She soon recovered her strength, but her sleep was often filled with nightmares, and the torment of her days in the mountains began showing itself in strange ways. She seldom finished all of her meals, always slipping something into her pocket to take back to her room: a piece of bread, a little fruit, or some dried beans from the kitchen. She hid these in a small tin box.

Mrs. Branham found her studying her stash one day. "Why, Lovina darling, whatever are you keeping this for? We've plenty more where that came from, and you're more than welcome to anything you need."

"I know, Mrs. Branham, but I…I keep thinking about the times when where wasn't enough…that I should be prepared in case…" and her voice trailed off.

Mrs. Branham put her arms around her and for the first time, Lovina let herself pour her heart out to her new friend.

Mrs. Branham gently comforted her and listened sympathetically as Lovina told about all of the horrors she had seen, the snow, the fear, the hunger, the deaths.

The older woman knew that Lovina needed to tell this story and that the best help she could give was just to listen.

When Lovina had finished, Mrs. Branham held her quietly and helped her dry her tears. Then she took Lovina by the hand and led her to the door.

"Come out here, dear," she said. "Maybe a little fresh air will make you feel better." She had noticed Lovina's interest in one of the young horses on the ranch. "Would you like to take her out for a ride?"

Lovina brightened at the offer. Perhaps a change of scene would help.

"Oh, Mrs. Branham, could I?"

"Well of, course, Vine. Patch is a gentle horse. I'm sure she'd like to have you take her out."

As they walked together out to the barn where the Western saddles were kept, Lovina wondered how she would be able to straddle the horse with her long skirts hanging to her ankles.

Mrs. Branham saw the puzzled look on her face. "Is something wrong?"

"I've never ridden a Western saddle with these petticoats before," she said. "What will I do with my skirts?"

Before Mrs. Branham could answer, Lovina had an idea. She bent over, reached between her legs for the back of her skirt and pulled it forward. Then she tucked it into her waistband, making the skirt into pantaloons.

Now she could climb onto the saddle and ride comfortably. Mrs. Branham laughed when she saw how her clever young friend had solved her problem.

Lovina loved the good times she had riding Patch through the fields with her long hair flying behind her, and she rode whenever she had the chance.

Pueblo life was never boring. The mission priest loved music and had taught the Indians to play many European instruments. Everyone at the presidio waited eagerly for the violin and French horn concerts that were held in the mission chapel every month.

Lovina attended school in the mornings, and helped Mrs. Branham in the house in the afternoon. She was getting to be a pretty fair cook, and was even learning to sew. In her spare time she wrote letters to Sarah and Ellen.

Best of all, she loved to play the little piano that was

kept in the parlor at the presidio. The music made her think of happier times. She wished she could still have her lessons with Aunt Mary, but she was surprised at how much she remembered and could still play by heart. Of course *Home Sweet Home* was still her favorite.

After she had been with the Branhams for a few months Lovina became friends with Virginia, the daughter of the presidio captain. Virginia was just about Lovina's age and the two girls enjoyed many of the same things. But Virginia had heard the gossip about how the Donner party had survived in the mountains and was curious to know about it first hand. Lovina found her new friend's questions painful to answer and began to find excuses not to spend time with her.

"What's the matter, Vine?" asked Virginia one day. "Why are you avoiding me?"

"It's nothing," answered Lovina.

"It must be something," Virginia went on. "You never want to do anything with me any more."

"Well, if you must know," said Lovina, as she turned and looked directly into Virginia's eyes, "it's all the questions you ask! I don't think you understand—I just don't want to talk about my family or the Donner Party any more!" and she turned and left her friend standing in the middle of the room.

"Well, I never…" Virginia stammered. "I…I really didn't mean to pry."

But the damage was done. Although Lovina and Ellen had never been forced to eat human flesh, they couldn't bear to think about what the others had faced, and Lovina chose to spend time alone rather than face the scorn of those who had heard those terrible stories.

From time to time, Mrs. Branham took her to visit Nancy. Lovina worried about her younger sister and the awful nightmares and crying spells the ten-year-old was still having. Nancy was among the last to be rescued and had seen the worst.

"Would it help if you told me about what happened after we all left and you and Mother were on your own up there?" Lovina asked one day.

"But, Vine, I just…I just don't want to think about it…," and Nancy began to cry. "I'm sorry, I try to be brave, but sometimes I just can't help it."

"Oh, Nancy, you cry all you need to. I'm here for you. I just thought maybe it would help if you talked about it."

"Well. I really can't remember very much, Vine. It seems like it was a terrible dream. We were all so hungry and cold and tired. Most of the time we just wrapped ourselves up and slept—until the pains woke us up. I just remember Momma handing me something warm to eat once in a while. I never asked her what it was. And then we'd go back to sleep again."

"Oh, my poor darling, Nancy!" and Lovina, too, began to cry.

The girls desperately missed their family. Lovina thought every day about her sisters' promise to send for her. She was impatient to join them in the Napa valley and ran excitedly for the mailbag each week, anxious for their letters.

She was twelve and still growing when she came to live with the Branhams, and even though she was thin and small for her age, her old clothes soon no longer fit her. The women at the presidio gave her some of their hand-me-downs, but most of the things she wore were old and faded. She hadn't been with the Branhams long when Mrs. Branham began to take notice of Lovina's sad wardrobe. Perhaps she had just the thing to warm a young girl's heart.

"Why, sakes alive, child, we can't have you growing up looking like a ragamuffin," she said one morning as they were dusting the bedroom.

"What if you get yourself invited to a party one day? You know, I have a dress that I brought with me from back East when Sam and I moved out here. Goodness knows it doesn't fit me any more. It might just fit you. And I'll bet the color will be beautiful with your eyes. You'll be needing something pretty to wear before long."

Mrs. Branham's eyes twinkled as she opened the big leather trunk under the window in Lovina's room and held up the lovely blue brocade.

Lovina couldn't believe her eyes. The dress was more beautiful than anything she had ever seen. She couldn't wait to try it on. It was a little too big and needed some mending here and there, but with Mrs. Branham's help, they soon had it looking like it was made for her. Lovina really couldn't wait to show her sisters! She hoped they'd send for her soon.

16

A Letter At Last

At last, one day in the spring of 1849, the eagerly-awaited news came. Ellen had moved to Napa from Sonoma, and she and Sarah were ready for Lovina to join them. She could leave next week on the stage going north.

She was a little worried about what to tell Nancy. When Mrs. Branham drove her to see her sister the next day, she hardly knew how to break the news.

"Oh, Nancy, darling, I hate to leave you like this, but I promise to write often. And I'm sure we'll be back to visit as soon as we can."

"Don't worry about me, Vine. I'll be fine," she said. "But you will let me know how you are, won't you?"

Mrs. Branham had become like a second mother to Lovina. She knew she could talk to her friend about almost anything, but she had not yet told her about her fear of water. She'd heard stories about the great San Francisco Bay and the crossing they'd have to make over the Carquinez Straits on their way north. She had visions of another raging torrent and was terrified at the thought of the ferry waiting for her.

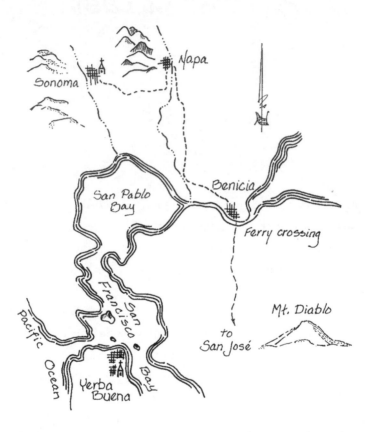

"You're so quiet, Vine," Mrs. Branham said as she was helping her pack her things. "Is there something I can help you with?"

Mrs. Branham had become very close to her young friend by this time, and knew something was bothering her.

"Oh, Mrs. Branham!" Lovina was in tears.

Mrs. Branham reached out her arms and pulled her close. "What's the matter, dear?"

Somehow things didn't look so bad with Mrs. Branham's arms around her. She poured out the long story: crossing the flooded rivers on the prairies, falling into the river in the mountains, fishing on the lake, living under all that heavy snow, and now her fear of the deep water they'd have to cross on the way to Sonoma.

Mrs. Branham smiled. "Well, Vine, let's talk about this. First of all, it's not like the raging rivers you've seen before at all. You'll be crossing the Carquinez Straits, where the Sacramento and San Joaquin Rivers come together and join San Francisco Bay.

"The strait is wide and deep, but mostly the water is on its way out to the bay and the ocean. When the tide is coming in, the water hardly moves at all. It's only when the tide is outbound that there's a current.

"You have absolutely nothing to worry about, dear. The ferry captains on the bay and the rivers are all experienced, and I have never heard of them losing one of their boats. Let's see now, maybe we can think of something that will help you when the time comes."

She closed her eyes for a few minutes, her brow knitted. Mrs. Branham guessed that Lovina's fear probably had nothing to do with water at all, but with all the horrors that she had seen in her young life.

"I have an idea," she said at last. "Remember the coin that you told me about? The one your mother gave you in the mountains? Well, I think it's a good-luck coin! It helped get you to Sutter's Fort safely, didn't it? I have a little purse you can put it in. Then you can carry it in your pocket where you can reach in and touch it when you're afraid. You'll know that your mother is there watching over you and guiding you on your way."

"Oh, Mrs. Branham, thank you—for everything!" Lovina hoped with all her heart the charm would work.

It was time to say good-bye to the family who had been so kind to her. Hardest of all was to leave the piano, and her dear friend, Patch, behind. The stagecoach would soon be here to take her to her new life with Sarah and Ellen in the Napa Valley.

17

Trial by Water

The weather was hot and the road dusty as they began their journey. Their stagecoach was one that made weekly trips between San José and the towns to the north. With her was a young family named Johnston, who were headed to the Mission San Francisco de Solano in Sonoma. Besides the mother and father, there were two pretty little girls, Meg and Amy. The children bounced and sang as they rode along and Lovina enjoyed their fun. It brought back happy memories of her childhood in Illinois.

She was excited to think she was finally going to be with her older sisters again. Best of all, they were going to arrive in Sonoma on July 3rd, her fifteenth birthday. What a good sign!

The California hills were brown in the heat of summer. Only the dark green oak trees offered shade, but she knew the fog would roll in at night to cool them off. Warm days, cool nights—no wonder the crops grew so well here in California!

The stagecoach headed east around the south end of San Francisco Bay and then turned north. Every little while Lovina put her hand in her pocket and touched her coin to reassure herself—still there. So far so good, she thought.

After they had rattled noisily through the pleasant countryside for several hours, the driver called back, "Time for lunch, folks. Want to stop here for a bit?" He pulled the stage over to the shade of a big oak tree and slowed to a stop.

They were all glad to climb down from the coach and stretch their legs. The ride had been bumpy and the children were getting tired. Mrs. Johnston brought out her basket and gave her family the lunch she had packed: chicken, cold potatoes and apples. Mrs. Branham had packed Lovina a lunch before she left, too, and her hard-boiled egg, biscuit and orange soon disappeared. She was surprised at how hungry she was. After a short stop, they were back on the road again. The straits shouldn't be far now.

As they came to the top of another brown hill the driver slowed the coach and called back, "Well, here we are folks!"

And there it was—the wide Carquinez Straits! They could see the ferryboat tied to a wooden dock. Although it didn't look very big from their hilltop, Mr. Johnston told her that besides passengers, the ferry carried loads of grain and other goods that had been shipped to the port of San Francisco and then on to the outlying areas.

There seemed to be a lot of activity going on down below. As the stagecoach drew closer, they could see men lifting large bundles onto the ferry's deck.

"This ferry's owned by Dr. Robert Semple, the founder of Benicia, Vine," said Mr. Johnston. "He's hoping they'll make Benicia the capital of California one day. He'll be a rich man if they do."

"Oh, Mr. Johnston," said Lovina, "I surely hope Dr. Semple knows as much about boats as he does politics!"

"What do you mean, Vine?"

"Well...I don't like water, or boats. Do you think we'll be all right?"

"Why of course, my dear. Now would I be taking my own family on this ferry if I didn't think it was safe?"

"I suppose not," Lovina had to admit.

"Then you just be brave. We'll be fine. You'll see."

The boatmen were soon ready to load the passengers. Lovina could put it off no longer. She walked slowly over to the gangplank and inched her way onto the boat deck where she held tightly to the railing. She closed her eyes and held on to her coin.

"Oh, please," she prayed, "let this be over soon." She could feel her chest tighten and her heart pounding.

"The captain has waited for high tide, when the water moves the slowest," called Mr. Johnston. "Looks like we'll have smooth sailing. Hop down here, girls. You can see how the men untie the boat." He was a bright young father, eager to have his children learn all about the world around them.

The strait was wide, and they could feel the pull of the current as the heavily-loaded boat slowly eased out into mid stream. Lovina wondered where they would end up if the captain couldn't hold his course.

The Johnston girls clearly enjoyed the river crossing and thought it was a great adventure. When Lovina finally dared take a quick peek, she could see that the ferry was out in the middle of the river. Mrs. Johnston stood next to her and Lovina could see worry in her eyes, too. Maybe she was reminded of some river crossings made on her own journey west.

Thankfully the water was calm and smooth on this lovely summer day, and they sailed safely across to the northern shore. Lovina hadn't moved a muscle the whole way.

As the ferry was unloaded and Vine could finally breathe again, she allowed herself to look back at the water. She touched her coin.

"Thank you, Mother," she whispered.

Mr. Johnston made arrangements for them to take the next stagecoach leaving for Sonoma. This last part of the trip took them over the lower delta of the Napa River and on to the Sonoma presidio and the mission. Like San José, the town was primarily a garrison, housing men, horses and supplies.

"Only about a day's ride separates each of the California missions, Vine, so there's lots of visitors coming and going between them," explained Mr. Johnston as they came closer to the mission. "Folks here are real friendly. Our family's

Sonoma Mission

looking forward to having a good time while we're here."

"Sounds wonderful," replied Lovina, "but I can't wait to see Ellen and Sarah. I wonder if they'll remember it's my birthday. Just seeing them will be the best present I could ask for! Now, where are they?"

The coach slowed down as they came to the square in the center of town. Lovina looked around and saw men, women and children going about their business. One of the men standing nearby looked like someone she knew, but where were her sisters? They didn't seem to be there waiting for her!

"Do you suppose my letter never arrived?" she wondered aloud to her new friends.

"Well," she decided, "I told them I was grown up, that I'm big enough to take care of myself. Guess I'd better prove it. You did say these folks were friendly, didn't you?"

"Are you sure you'll be all right?" asked Mrs. Johnston.

"I'll be fine, thanks," answered Lovina. "In fact, I think I know that man standing over there by those wagons. Do you think I should speak to him?" She climbed down from the coach and stepped closer.

"Could I be of help?" he asked.

She smiled shyly and curtsied.

"Pardon me, sir, but I've just arrived in town on the stagecoach and my family doesn't seem to be here to meet me. They're from the Napa Valley and I wonder if you know how I might catch a ride over there?"

He gave her a warm smile. "Well now, young lady, I'm headed that way myself," he answered. "You're more than welcome to ride along with me, but I can't say as you'll be very comfortable on my old buckboard. It's not outfitted for passengers. Look here, child, don't I know you?"

"My name's Lovina Graves, and my sisters are Sarah Fosdick and Ellen Graves. Do you know them?"

The old man's smile grew wider. "Well, of course I do. And I remember you, too. My name's Reason Tucker. I headed up the rescue party that went into the mountains to

bring you youngsters out a couple of years back. Why, I'd
never have recognized you, Lovina. You've grown into quite
a young lady."

"Oh, Mr. Tucker, what a wonderful surprise! I thought
you looked familiar. I'm so glad to meet you again. If it hadn't
been for you and your men, none of us would be alive today.
We owe you so many thanks!" Her eyes filled with tears as
the memories of those terrible days came rushing back to
her.

"Well, child, once we heard about you, we had no choice.
We couldn't just stand by and leave you up there to die. It
could just as easily have been one of us.

"Isn't this just dandy that we've met up again like this?
You asked if I know your sisters? Well I surely do. Sarah's
been stayin' on with our neighbors, the Kelloggs, for near
two years now. Fine girl she is, too! Been teachin' the young
ones in a little school she's set up in the shanty in front of
Dr. Bale's grist mill."

They started across the square. "Oh, and of course your
sister Ellen's there now, too. Pretty as a picture she is. Won't
they be surprised to see you! Here, let me help you up and
we'll be on our way. Napa's not far." He took her small valise
and set it in the wagon.

And so, on July 3, 1849, Miss Lovina Graves and Mr.
Reason Tucker set out together once more, this time on
their way to the Napa Valley, and home.

Mr. Tucker was right about his wagon: It was a bumpy
ride. The buckboard had only a hard seat high up in front
and wasn't built for comfort, but Lovina didn't care. She
was finally going to be with her family, and at the end of her

long, long journey. She was nearly home at last.

The summer day was hot and the trip took them over rough, dusty roads for about fifteen miles. Although her face was dirty and her dress clung to her back, Lovina would remember it as the best ride of her life.

"Is this really the Napa Valley?" she cried as they came out into the wide basin at the lower end of the Napa River. She could hardly believe her eyes. She recalled hearing that someone had described the valley as a great unfenced park.

"It's the most beautiful place I've ever seen!"

"This is it," Mr. Tucker replied.

Pines, firs, and red-barked madrones covered the surrounding hills, and stately oaks dotted the valley floor.

As they moved on into the valley, the wagon rattled past the tidewater and the wandering river. Clover, wild oats and wildflowers spread across the valley floor in a blanket of green and yellow. As she looked out at the shoulder-high grasses, she noticed a slight ripple. Suddenly, a large elk bounded across the road in front of the wagon.

"Steady now, boys," called Mr. Tucker as his startled horses began to rear. "Whoa there! Settle down, that's better." The horses soon returned to their gentle trot as they continued on their way. Lovina liked the way Mr. Tucker handled his animals.

"The stories my sisters have told me about all the game in these parts certainly appears to be true," said Lovina. "Do you think we'll see any grizzly or brown bears today? I've heard there are mountain lions that roam these hills, too."

"Oh, yes, Vine, this valley is home to many animals. We see lots of bears, but the lions keep pretty much to the higher mountains, unless we haven't had much rain and they come down looking for water. This is still pretty wild country. You never know where these animals are going to be. Just be careful. That's my best advice."

Lovina felt happier than she had in a long time. Mr. Tucker had rescued her for the second time, and they were becoming fast friends.

The site of George Yount's first dwelling,
a Kentucky blockhouse built like a fort,
is marked by a monument on Yount
Mill Road, north of Yountville.

18

Together Again

They had traveled about eight or ten miles north into the valley when Mr. Tucker pointed to a large farm off in the distance.

"That's the home of George Yount, Vine," he told her.

"Oh, I've heard about Captain Yount," Lovina said. "He was one of the first settlers here, wasn't he?"

"That's right," he continued, "Yount came here to the valley in 1831. He married a Spanish lady and got himself a large land grant from Mexico. It's called the Caymus Rancho. They say it helps to get the best land if you marry someone from Spain, because the Spanish government figures this'll keep out other foreigners. I should have married one myself I guess, but I didn't think the missus would take too kindly to that idea." He chuckled at his own little joke, and then he went on.

"George Yount, you see, is a close friend of General Vallejo, and those two fellas spend a lot of time visitin' back and forth. The Captain knows just about everybody in these parts. He's built himself a fine two-story house and he welcomes most all the newcomers to his home to stay until they get settled.

"Besides, there's some pretty ornery grizzlies around here, and good hunters are always needed. Well now, here we are," said Mr. Tucker as he turned off into the Yount's drive.

As the wagon came rattling into the Yount's front yard, young John Cyrus looked out from the barn to see what all the noise was about. John was a teen-ager himself, and when he saw this strange girl about his own age sitting on Mr. Tucker's rig, he shyly ducked back behind the buildings.

There was something different about this girl. Perhaps it was her way of looking directly at him, with just about the bluest eyes he had ever seen. She looked familiar, but he knew that the Tuckers had no daughters. Who was she?

Lovina had seen him too and wondered who this nice-looking young man was. Though their meeting was brief, she hoped she'd get to see him again.

John's father, Enoch Cyrus, and his family had been in the valley only a short time themselves. They had been invited to stay on with the Younts until they could find a place of their own. Extra hands were always needed to help farm Yount's land, and the Cyrus men were known as skilled hunters.

"Hello there, Reason," said Captain Yount. "Who's your passenger? My goodness, child, hop down off that rig and stretch your legs. You don't look very comfortable up there.

"Don't know as I've seen you around here before, Miss. I'm George Yount." He offered her his hand.

"Good afternoon," smiled Lovina.

Mr. Tucker jumped down from his seat and strode up to Captain Yount. The men shook hands.

"Good afternoon, George. Have a look here. Doesn't this pretty young lady look like someone you've seen before?"

"Hmm." Yount thought for a moment and then smiled. "Well now, of course! I'll bet you're one of the Graves girls, right? You sure are! Darned if you don't look just like your sister, Ellen."

"Yes, sir," she said, "I'm Lovina Graves, but everyone calls me Vine. I've been living down in San José for the past two years. My sisters have asked me to come to live with them here in the valley now. Mr. Tucker and I have known each other for a long time."

Yount shook his head and looked sadly down at her.

"Yes," he sighed, "I know all about you girls. We were mighty sorry to hear about you folks who were stranded there in the mountains. Took out a company myself to see if we could help, but by the time we got there, it was too late."

He shook his head, "Terrible thing, just terrible!"

Then a warm smile crossed his rugged face. "Now come on in, child; you look like you could use some rest."

Lovina was relieved to see that Captain Yount didn't appear to be disturbed by the terrible stories he must surely have heard.

He showed her into the house and introduced her to his wife.

"Welcome to our home, Lovina," she said. Mrs. Yount

took her upstairs to a small bedroom with a window looking out over the valley below.

As she looked out past the big oak tree standing in the yard, Lovina's eyes filled with tears. She remembered her father leading the wagons over the plains, and thought about how amazed they had been at the beauty of the wind-swept land. It seemed like only yesterday, and here she was at last, in this lovely valley. Franklin Graves would have loved this place.

"I think your sisters may have a surprise in store for you, Lovina," Mrs. Yount told her. "I understand Ellen's been seeing quite a bit of that young McDonnell fellow since she's moved in with Sarah. They say there might be a wedding soon."

A wedding! I'll bet they waited for me to come to surprise me, she thought. This was wonderful news!

"Now make yourself comfortable, dear," Mrs. Yount continued. "I'll just go back downstairs and make some tea. Call me if you need anything."

Lovina lay down on the narrow bed, closed her eyes and before long, she was sound asleep. It had been a long day.

When she awoke, Mrs. Yount had tea waiting. "Can I help you unpack, dear?"

"Oh, thank you," replied Lovina. "I would like to press my good dress. Could I use your irons?"

"Of course, dear. I'll just go on down and get them warmed up for you."

Lovina hadn't brought much with her. She took out her comb, brush, and change of clothes which she laid on the small bureau. Then she carefully unfolded the dress Mrs. Branham had sent with her. She took it down to the kitchen where Mrs. Yount had the irons heating on the old wood stove.

"What a beautiful gown, Lovina. It's just the color of your eyes!" she exclaimed.

"Oh, thank you, Mrs. Yount," said Lovina. "It was one of Mrs. Branham's. I never guessed when we were working on it that I'd have a chance to wear it so soon. And now, if there's going to be a wedding, I'll be all ready!"

She carefully arranged the dress on the big ironing board, and began to press out the wrinkles, changing from one iron to another as they cooled.

"Do you suppose I could leave it with you for a while, Mrs. Yount?"

"Of course, my dear," smiled Mrs. Yount. "Why this is too elegant to be carting around all over the countryside," and she gave Lovina a knowing smile.

That night, as Lovina lay in the small bed, thinking over all that had happened to her, she could hardly believe that she was finally here. And tomorrow she would get to see Sarah and Ellen!

News traveled fast in the valley. Early the next morning, her sisters hitched the horses up to the Kelloggs' buggy and arrived at the Yount ranch by mid-morning. Lovina ran to meet them, smiling from ear to ear. They were together at last!

"Oh, Vine!" cried Ellen, "We didn't know you were coming so soon. I can't believe it's really you! And look, Sarah, look at how grown up she is!"

Lovina's letter had never arrived.

After they warmly thanked the Younts, the girls started back up the valley to the little cabin which Mr. Kellogg had built for Sarah near the grist mill.

It had been over two years since they had been together. There was a lot of catching up to do and the older girls were anxious to hear about Nancy.

Lovina pretended to be surprised when Ellen told her about Bill McDonnell and the wedding they were planning. Bill had been a team driver for the Kellogg family when they came from the East two years earlier. There were not many eligible young women in the valley, so matches were made quickly. Lovina wondered what a wedding in this new land would be like.

One of the first people she asked about was their brother, Will. "Did he make the trip into the mountains safely? Did he find the coins?"

"Yes, he made it back safely, but I'm afraid he didn't find any sign of the money," said Sarah. "Nobody knows what happened to it. He went back to Illinois after that and then returned to California. Will hasn't been around here for several months now. He spends a lot of his time talking to folks about what happened when we were up in the mountains."

"What do you mean, Sarah?" Lovina was curious.

"Well, I think Will's tired of all the wild stories that are being circulated about the Donner Party," said Sarah. "Folks are curious about the trouble we had, but most of them hear only the stories that are told from James Reed's point of view."

"Mr. Reed's point of view?" Lovina was puzzled.

Sarah went on, "Oh, yes, he's had a lot to say about what happened to us. But remember, Vine, Mr. Reed was banished and was separated from the rest of us long before we ever got trapped in those mountains. He wasn't even there with us when the food gave out and everyone began to starve.

"Will says Reed's stories make everyone seem pretty foolish. Will worked side by side with those men, and he wants people to understand that they did the best they could, that they really were brave.

"Ellen and I would like to have him forget all this and stay here with us, but he's got strong opinions, and he can't seem to put it all behind him. We know better than to argue with him."

"Oh, Sarah," Lovina sighed. "We're alive and well, and lucky to be here. Can't we just forget the past and get on with our lives?"

"I'm afraid not, Vine," said her sister. "It's not that easy. None of us will ever forget what happened up there. We shouldn't. You just can't forget the friends and family you lost. Whatever we do, it's going to be part of our lives forever.

This may just be Will's way of putting his nightmares to rest. You're still young, honey. Maybe you'll understand more when you're older."

That night, Lovina thought for a long time about her mother and father, her family, and the old farm in Illinois. She could remember clearly how their journey began: she could picture the prairies, the Wasatch mountains, the Great Salt Desert, and everything about her life with the Branhams. But the entrapment in the mountains? She couldn't seem to bring those scenes into focus. Her mind wanted to shut out those terrible times.

As she drifted off to sleep and thought about all the things that had happened, she began to softly hum *Home Sweet Home*. She just knew that California was going to be the home she longed for.

19

Life in the Valley

The three of them were crowded in Sarah's small cabin. The beds took up most of the floor space and there was barely room for a table, but they were happy just to be together. It reminded Lovina and Ellen of the times they used to play house under the big trees in back of the cabin in Illinois.

There were always letters to write to Nancy and Mary and the valley to explore, but Lovina spent most of her time taking care of her chores. Her days were filled with woman's work—washing, ironing clothes, cooking meals or tending the garden. What was that her mother used to say? Something about women's work never being done.

They'd been hoping Ellen and Bill would be married soon, but Bill wouldn't hear of a wedding without a suitable home for his bride. He had been saving every penny to build a new house on some land the United States government was offering to new settlers. The ceremony would have to wait until a proper home was built.

The valley was filled with fun-loving young men and women. Lovina loved the house parties she was invited to at the neighboring ranches, where there were quilting bees for the women and horse-breaking contests or hunting trips for the men to enjoy.

Edward T. Bale's Mill was a gathering spot for early settlers.

One morning early the next fall, Lovina stood listening to the bluejays arguing above her in the old oak tree next to the mill. She and Ellen had been helping Bill unload grain from his big wagon.

"Looks like we'll have enough flour from this load to last

us for some time, Ellen," Bill said. "Maybe I should sell some. Sure could use the extra money."

The girls gasped. Not keep every bit of what Bill had worked so hard to raise? It was hard for them to believe that they would really have enough food to last until the next year's crops were harvested. The memory of starvation was too near.

Lovina still saved everything that looked like it might be wasted. Beans, dried fruits, venison jerky, scraps of cloth, and all manner of odd items went into a box which she kept beneath her bed. She knew she would probably never use all the things she put there, but she couldn't help herself. She couldn't forget that terrible time in the mountains when they had nothing.

As the girls were walking to the cabin one afternoon, Dr. Bale, the owner of the mill, drove by in his carriage.

"Afternoon ladies," he called. "Going to the big dance next week?"

Ellen smiled and waved, "Oh yes, Dr. Bale, we wouldn't miss it."

Sarah and Ellen had been invited to these parties at the Sonoma Presidio before, but this would be Lovina's first dance, and she was getting nervous.

"I haven't been to Sonoma since last summer," said Lovina to Ellen a little later. She was beginning to wonder if this was really going to be such a good idea. She hadn't ever been to a real dance, and she worried that she might step on her partner's toes.

"Don't worry, Vine," Ellen answered. "It'll be fun, you'll see."

The trip was to last for several days. The girls would stay in the home of some of the Kellogg's friends.

"Tell me again about Sonoma and the presidio, Sarah," said Lovina. "Why are there so many soldiers there?"

"Well, it all started when the settlers took the presidio from the Mexicans earlier this year. That was when the 'Bear Flag Republic' was born. The Bear Flag only flew for twenty-

California Bear Flag ~ 1846

five days, and then it was replaced by the Stars and Stripes and California finally became part of the United States.

"The capital's been moved to Monterey now, but some folks think it should be returned to Sonoma. Everyone's so excited about California becoming a state—they want the capital back in Sonoma, where it all began. There's a lot of fighting still going on."

"No wonder there are so many soldiers there," said Lovina. "There won't be any shooting, will there?"

"No, no, silly. I meant they were arguing about it. Tempers are running high, but I think the warring is over. The U.S. troops were here to fight the war with Mexico—and to protect us from outsiders—not each other," she went on. "Now, are you coming with us or not?"

"But what will I wear?" Lovina worried. She had been saving Mrs. Branham's dress for Ellen's wedding and didn't want to spoil her surprise.

"My green dress should fit you, Vine," said Sarah. "I've just finished making up that blue striped material that Mrs. Tucker gave me for helping her out with her canning this fall, so I'll wear that."

Lovina finally agreed, but as she climbed up onto the Kellogg's wagon the next week, she was still nervous. She wondered if this really was such a good idea.

The party started early in the evening. There was a light buffet dinner first, which was followed by dancing. When the first young soldier came towards her she knew she'd made a terrible mistake. She couldn't dance! What would she talk about? She wished she'd stayed at home.

As it turned out, he had never danced much before either. "'Scuse me, miss. May I have this dance? I hope I don't step on your toes. I'm kinda new at this myself, but I'd sure like to give it a try." And before she knew it, she was on the dance floor, dancing and laughing and telling him all about Napa and her sisters.

She had a wonderful time. The men outnumbered the women by at least five to one and she was asked to dance every dance. She stepped on a lot of toes, but no one seemed to mind. None of her partners were such great dancers either.

She hoped she'd find John Cyrus in the crowd, but he didn't seem to have much interest in parties. His family had moved onto some land in Calistoga, and he was busy help-ing build the house and barns.

20

The Wedding

The following September, Bill McDonnell finally finished the house and at last the wedding plans could be made. Because the valley still had no church, the bride and groom would travel to Benicia, where a minister would perform the ceremony.

A wedding celebration was planned for their return. Lovina would have to wait a little longer to show off her beautiful dress.

"Hey, there, little sister," called Bill one morning as he and Ellen were saddling the horses. "How'd you like to come with us on our honeymoon trip?" Lovina could hardly believe her ears. Could he be serious?

She knew the newlyweds were planning to go south to San José to visit Nancy and then on to San Juan Bautista where Mary lived.

Lovina hesitated, "Oh, Bill, that would be wonderful, but you don't really want me along on your honeymoon, do you?"

"Listen here, Vine, we're all family now," he answered. "Ellen and I will have plenty of time alone together. We'd really like you to come with us."

"Oh yes, please come, Vine," Ellen begged. "Nancy and Mary will be so happy to see you. And we'll visit the Branhams, too."

"Well…let me think about it," Lovina hesitated. "We'd have to take the ferry, wouldn't we?" She could feel her chest tighten. She hadn't told them how frightened she'd been when she made the trip the first time.

Ellen remembered her sister's fears on the trail and understood Lovina's hesitation. "Please think about it, Vine. You'll be fine, won't she Bill?"

"Absolutely! We'll take good care of you. You'll see." He gave Lovina a big smile.

Oh, dear, Lovina thought. What should I do? I know I shouldn't be afraid to go, but what if I panic again? I'd be so embarrassed. She worried and fussed for several more days, and finally agreed. She would do it. This reunion was too important to miss. She would manage somehow.

On the day of the wedding, they awakened at dawn. Lovina dressed and packed her bag. Then she took out her mother's coin and held it tightly in her hand. She was going to make this trip! The magic of the coin had worked before; she hoped it would work again. She quietly watched as Bill saddled their horses. Sarah would go as far as Benicia with them, but she would have to return home the next day to her students.

When the time came to leave, they mounted their horses, waved good-bye to all their friends and started down the trail, past the new city of Napa, and on to Benicia. The sun was shining, the birds were singing. It was a beautiful day and they were off to a wedding.

The ceremony that was held that evening in the small new Methodist church was short and simple—just Ellen, Bill, Lovina, Sarah and the minister. Following the service, the wedding party checked into the hotel in the center of town and treated themselves to a fine dinner in the hotel restaurant.

The next morning, Sarah waited as the bride, groom and new sister-in-law gathered their things together. Then she followed them down to the dock where Bill began loading the horses. It was another lovely day, but Sarah could see that something wasn't quite right. Lovina stood off by herself, staring at the ferryboat rocking in the water.

"What's the matter, Vine?" Sarah asked.

Lovina didn't answer.

"Vine?"

"I don't think I can go, Sarah."

"Can't go? What do you mean, you can't go? Of course you're going! Now you just get yourself on that ferryboat right now. Everyone's waiting for you." Sarah knew that if she let Lovina back out now, she would never get over this fear.

Lovina's heart sank. How could she let everybody down

like this? She wanted so much to take this trip with Ellen and Bill, but she couldn't make herself move. She felt as if someone had tied her shoes to the ground.

Just then, Bill came striding up, swooped her up in his arms, and giving a loud whoop, lifted her onto the deck. "There now, dear lady, we're all set!" How could she get off now!

"Oh, Bill," she laughed, "what am I going to do with you? You're a case, you really are!" But inside she silently thanked him. If it weren't for Ellen's new husband, she would still be standing there on the dock. Maybe this voyage wouldn't be so bad after all. Having a man around was wonderful.

She grasped the coin in her pocket, closed her eyes, smiled, and said a little prayer.

The boat moved smoothly out onto the water, turned and headed to the other shore. Ellen stood on one side of her and Bill on the other, pointing out several large boats and some interesting water birds just ahead. As long as she didn't look down into the water she was all right, and they soon found themselves safe on the other side. Not too bad, Lovina thought. I'm doing better.

After they'd landed and taken the horses ashore, they headed south through the rolling hills. There was so much to talk about as they rode along, so much that had happened since they'd come to California: the new friends, the wonderful weather, and now, the new statehood, that the time flew by.

When daylight began to fade and the trail got harder to see, they looked for a place to spend the night. Near a small stream with some overhanging willows they dismounted, unsaddled their horses and turned them loose to drink and graze. The biscuits, venison jerky and crisp apples they'd brought with them made a fine supper. Using their saddles as pillows, the three were soon fast asleep.

When they awoke the next morning, a light rain was falling. So much for the lovely California weather!

"Better get moving," called Bill. They hurriedly packed up their belongings and headed westward, following the stream until they came to a trail that turned south.

"Do you think this is the right way?" asked Ellen.

"Who cares, darlin'? We're off to see the world!" and her new husband laughed his hearty laugh. They were having so much fun on their great adventure they didn't even mind the rain. They knew Bill wouldn't let them get lost.

"Well look at that!" declared Bill. As he spoke, the clouds parted and a beautiful rainbow spread across the sky before them. "Good sign, ladies, good times ahead!"

The morning air was warm and fresh as the travelers continued southward through the lovely San Ramon Valley, past Mission San José, and on to the pueblo where the Branhams were anxiously waiting for them to arrive.

"Oh, Vine, we're so glad you've come too!" cried Mrs. Branham. "We've missed you! Come in, come in! Your rooms are all ready for you! Now tell us all about Napa."

The next morning, after breakfast, Lovina asked about Patch. "So you still have him? Could I take him for a ride?"

Mr. Branham chuckled. "Well now, Vine, let's just have a look. I certainly wouldn't want to disappoint my favorite girl."

Patch whinnied and nuzzled her with her soft nose when

Lovina came into the barn. "Hello there, old friend," she seemed to say.

After such a long trip, the Branham family insisted they stay on for a while. Bill helped Mr. Branham with the new barn he was building, and the girls visited with Nancy, Mary, and her new husband.

Lovina had often wondered how her sisters answered the prying questions they must have been asked about the Donner Party over the years. She wished they would talk about their feelings, but she didn't want to open a subject that would bring back painful memories, so she remained quiet and waited for an opening.

At last an opportunity came one day while the girls were cleaning up after lunch. Nancy began to hum to herself as she carried the dishes to the kitchen sink.

"Isn't that *Home Sweet Home* you're humming, Nancy?" asked Lovina.

"Well, yes, I guess it is," answered Nancy. "It always reminds me of you, Vine, when I think of that song."

"Me, too," said Mary. "Remember how Lovina and Ellen kept trying to remember all the verses on the trail?"

The girls stopped what they were doing and looked at each others' faces.

"Who would have thought that we would ever have gone through that horror and still end up safely here in California after all?" said Mary. With that, they put their arms around each other and soon they were all in tears.

"Do people still ask you about the mountains?" asked Lovina.

Nancy and Mary looked at each other. Lovina wondered

if they had ever talked about this with each other?

Nancy cleared her throat. "They sometimes do, but the people who have become our friends understand that it's not something we want to be reminded of. It's taken us a long time to get on with our lives here, but people are still curious. Some seem to feel we're heroes, but I think there are others who still think we did something unforgivable, don't you agree, Mary?"

"Yes, I'm afraid you're right, Nancy. Sarah and I should probably tell the story of the Snowshoe Party, too, some day. But I don't think anyone believes that we girls could have survived in the snow while most of the men died. I just know that when Father and Jay died, I thought that was the end for all of us. Who would have thought that the women would be the stronger ones in the party?"

Everyone was silent. At last Ellen spoke up, "Well, girls, we've got work to do here. Let's get busy with these dishes." The conversation was over.

Lovina was so proud of her sisters. She knew that at no time in history had women endured more than they had. There was work to do and they were happy to be doing it.

It was nearly a month before they started back to Napa. When they returned, it was time to plan for the wedding celebration. Everyone joined in the excitement. The women spent days preparing their favorite dishes. Cakes and pies, roast turkeys, baked sweet potatoes and venison roasts would be served, as well as a handsome wedding cake that Sarah made from flour ground at Dr. Bale's mill. Long tables were set up under the oak trees not far from Ellen and Bill's new house.

Lovina was so excited she could hardly wait. She was staying with Ellen and Bill so she could help them get settled. Earlier in the week she had ridden down to the Yount's on the pretense of gathering some black walnuts that grew by the creek. Mrs. Yount helped wrap her dress in brown paper and lay it over the back of her saddle. She took the long way back home, along the western hills to avoid meeting any of her family on the main road.

"If I run into a bear on this trip I don't know what I'll do," she thought, "but I've waited too long to wear this dress to have anything spoil my surprise! Out of the way, bears! Here I come!"

Fortunately there were no wandering animals out that afternoon. When she reached home, Ellen was busy making decorations. Lovina ran quickly into the house and hid her dress under the bed.

On Sunday afternoon, when everyone began to gather, Lovina slipped into the house to retrieve her treasure. As she eased it over her head, she gasped! The dress didn't fit her anymore! She hadn't reached her full size when she was at the Branhams' and now she couldn't even fasten the buttons!

Oh, no! What would she do?

At just that moment, Sarah came into the house to pick up something for the party. When she saw Lovina in her fancy dress with tears streaming down her cheeks, her heart went out to her. "Why, Vine," she cried, "where did you get that beautiful gown?"

"Oh, Sarah, what am I going to do?" she cried. "Mrs. Branham gave it to me when I was living with them, but that was over a year ago, and now it doesn't fit me! We worked so hard to make it just right! What will I do? I've been planning to surprise you all for such a long time."

"Oh, my sweet, don't you worry. I think I can help," replied Sarah. "You just wait right there."

With that, Sarah darted out the door and down to her little cabin at the end of the road. She was back in no time with a bundle under her arm.

"Lovina Graves," she said, "it's time you found out what it's like to be a woman." And she unrolled something her sister had seen, but never worn—a corset!

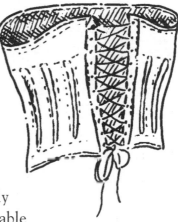

"I can't breathe," Lovina gasped, as Sarah laced her in. "Hold on, silly!" said her sister. "We'll have you into this dress in no time!"

When they finally had her squeezed into the painful waist cincher, they tried the dress on again. It fit like a glove.

"But I can't say I like it," said Lovina. "I can hardly breathe, and I'll surely not be able to eat a mouthful."

"Sorry," said Sarah, "but you'll get used to it. If you'd stayed back in Marshall County, you'd probably be wearing one of these every single day."

"Now I know we made the right decision when we came west!" Lovina laughed.

How surprised everyone was when she stepped out in

her new dress. Ellen cried, "Why, Vine, you don't look like the same girl we saw just a few minutes ago! You're all grown up! Where have you been keeping this beautiful gown?"

Lovina told her how she'd brought the dress with her from San José and all about the fun she'd had hiding it until she could surprise them. Sarah could hardly keep a straight face.

21

Bears, Pigs and More Bears

Lovina stayed on in the new house with Ellen and Bill after they married, and most days she walked down the hill in the morning to help Sarah.

The wild animals frequently came down near the ranch and Lovina would often see fresh tracks of small animals in the damp path. Occasionally larger prints told her that a grizzly had passed that way the night before.

Hogs had been introduced into the valley by now, and every farm had a few pigs. The bears loved pig meat and had become a serious threat to the farm animals. The small piglets were easy to catch, so the farmers had built sturdy sheds to shut them in at night.

Locking the pigs in for the night was one of Lovina's chores. One evening, however, she missed a young piglet and he was left outside to wander about. Bill was gone on a hunting trip, and Lovina and Ellen were home alone. They had not gone to bed yet when a prowling grizzly came wandering by and discovered the unfortunate pig, who of course tried to run to the house for protection. If Bill had been home, or if he'd left his rifle at the house, they might have been able to save the poor animal, but Bill had taken his guns with him and the women were home alone without a weapon.

The bear chased the pig around and around the house. Each time they came near the door, the girls would yell and

wave their arms wildly at the bear, trying to drive him away, but the best they could do was force him to run in a wider circle. Each time he circled the house, the pig ran past the door with the bear close behind. This went on until the bear finally succeeded in heading his prey away from the building. That was the end of the pig.

"That does it," muttered Bill when he returned. "That bear's got to go!"

Grizzlies often killed young cattle as well as hogs. The bears had become such a problem that hunts were often organized to try to get rid of them.

Before the pigs were introduced, bear fat made a good substitute for lard, which the settlers used for making candles. The tough bear meat wasn't as tasty as the deer and elk that were so plentiful, but the hides made warm blankets, rugs and moccasins.

After the rest of the men returned from their hunt and heard the latest pig story, they decided to take action.

The big bear, the one who had "gotten away with the bacon" many times, was one of the biggest grizzlies ever seen in the area. Only a few days earlier, old Hog Killer, as he had become known, had shown up at the Nashes', where he'd been trying to tear off the roof of the pig pen. Poor old Mr. Nash was such a poor shot he merely chased the bear away!

The grizzly next stopped at the Owsleys' place on Mark West Springs Road. Mr. Owsley was as good a shot as any, but rifles in those days were not always dependable, and this one wasn't working properly. The bear, not waiting to give him a chance to take aim again, headed to the Kilburn's farm.

The Kilburn's log house stood near two large oaks. A mother pig had made her bed with her babies between the trees in the front yard. Mr. Kilburn thought they would surely be safe so near the house, so he didn't put them in the crowded pen with the other pigs that night.

Now, farmhouses meant nothing to old Hog Killer. When he smelled a piglet, he would take one right off the door-step, if necessary. This time he started after the brood between the  trees and the front door. The mother pig put up a terrible fight. Old man Kilburn, hearing the squeals, jumped to the rescue, but he had loaned his rifle to a friend and had only a weak "pepper-box" six-shooter left for a weapon.

The gun fired but wasn't powerful enough to pierce the tough hide of the bear and only served to drive him away. He must have spent the rest of the day in the wooded hills nearby, because as afternoon approached, the farmers could hear him growling not far off, no doubt hungry for his next meal.

When he arrived at the Fowlers that afternoon, he found the only loose animal was the big old family boar. The bear began his attack. The boar was a tough old boy himself and was putting up a good fight when Mr. Fowler and his men appeared with their guns.

They had to be careful where they were shooting so they wouldn't hit the boar, and once again the bear escaped without a serious wound, this time heading up the canyon and back into the hills. The men followed at a short distance, but soon found it impossible to try to track him as the light of the afternoon sun began to fade. They returned to the house to plan a big hunt for the next day.

Early in the morning all the hog owners gathered and set off up the canyon in pursuit of their prey. Some of the men were good hunters, but not all were good shots.

The women had been up early too. As soon as the hunters were gone they began cooking and packing their baskets with picnic fare. This would be an occasion for a celebration if their men were successful. By now everyone in the valley had heard about the raids.

The first scattered group of bear hunters, who just happened to have more hog owners than sharpshooters in their midst, met the old boy face to face. They fired wild and wide. The noise so enraged the animal that he turned back and began chasing after the men! It was all they could do to get away.

Not long after, another group of hunters came upon a bear, only this time it wasn't the old grizzly, but a younger and smaller animal. After much shooting and yelling, they brought him down, but he was the wrong bear.

At last the hunters found the trail of old Hog Killer himself, and overtook him along the watershed between two streams that tumbled down the hills.

The grizzly took shelter in a brush patch, but with so much shouting and firing, he was soon forced to move on.

Just below his hiding place was a long slope. His only chance of escape was through the open space to the safety of the forest beyond.

What happened next astonished even the most experienced hunters. To get down the hill, this wily bear used a means of travel none of the men had ever seen before. He stood up, circled his head with his forepaws, and curling up his hind legs, rolled down the hill over and over, like a great brown ball.

With hunters stationed all around, each man had time to take his best shot at this rolling mass of fur on its trip down the hillside, but none appeared to hit the target and the bear kept on rolling.

At the bottom of the hill the big bear was stopped by some dogs who had been following his trail all morning. Grizzlies are not usually tree climbers, but when they are in danger, they will do whatever it takes to save themselves. The dogs soon chased him up into a tree, where he tried to hide among the leaves.

"We've got him trapped now, men," someone called. "Be careful not to hit one of the dogs! That bear's apt to jump down and start chasin' em."

"We'd better have one fella do the shootin'!" called Bill. That way we won't waste our ammunition. Hey there, John, get yourself up that tree!"

Young John Cyrus was pleased that the men thought he was a good enough shot to take on the bear. He was young and agile, and had already killed several bears on hunts with his father and brothers.

He scampered up into the tree next to the one in which the bear had taken refuge. As soon as he felt comfortable, he took careful aim and began to fire. The other men, standing below, reloaded their rifles and handed a fresh one up to him after each shot.

John sat on the branch of the tree shooting at the bear for several minutes, but nothing happened. What was wrong here? John knew he must have made some hits, but the bear stayed fast in the tree. Was he stuck there? At last, with a loud crash, the big animal tumbled to the ground, dead.

A great shout went up as the hunters gathered around to view their prize. The women and children, who had been watching from a safe distance, came running as well.

After everyone had a chance to look at this fallen giant, the hide was removed. That tough old boy proved to be the biggest grizzly ever taken in the area. He had 28 bullet holes in him! John had not been such a bad shot after all.

As soon as they had taken care of the bear's remains, everyone gathered at the mill to celebrate their victory. When lunch was served, John Cyrus found himself sitting at the same picnic table as Miss Lovina Graves. "What a good shot you are, John!" she said. "It must have been hard to keep your balance in that tree and hold onto the rifle at the same time. Weren't you afraid you'd fall?"

"Oh, it was nothin', Miss Graves," he answered shyly, "just another ol' bear hunt."

When he smiled she felt warm all over. She'd known all along she'd get to know him better one day, and it had been worth the wait.

Looking into her merry blue eyes, poor John was captivated. Was it he or Lovina who'd had a successful day's hunting?

22

Test of Courage

Not long after the bear hunt, a visitor arrived at the Cyrus family's door. He wasn't feeling well and asked if he might spend the night. It soon became apparent that the man was very ill.

Within days, Enoch Cyrus, his two older sons, his wife, daughter and young John were sick as well. A strict quarantine went into effect. Outsiders were forbidden to enter the house. Their visitor had brought smallpox to the valley.

When Lovina heard about the quarantine, she became worried that there was no one to care for John and his family. Someone had to help. Knowing no one would be allowed in the house to fix their meals, she went to her precious hoard. First she made a hearty soup and some biscuits. Then she took out a jar of the wild berry jam that she and Ellen had made last summer. She poured the soup into a small milk can with a tight-fitting lid and packed everything into a basket. Then she wrapped it all with a woolen shawl and climbed up onto one of Bill's horses. She nestled the basket on the saddle in front of her and set off.

The Cyrus family had settled nearby in Calistoga, so the trip wouldn't take long, but in her excitement she had forgotten about the recent rains.

The Napa River was normally a slow-moving stream which drained the rain waters from the nearby hills into San Pablo Bay. But sometimes, when the rains had been unusually heavy, the river flooded its banks and the settlers had to be cautious of how and where they traveled. This was one of those times.

As Lovina rushed out through the front gate, Bill came riding up on the farm wagon.

"Where are you going, Vine?"

"I'm taking some food to the Cyrus'," she yelled. It had begun to rain again, and she knew she would have to hurry to reach the bridge before dark.

"Are you crazy?" he shouted. "River's flooding up-valley. You shouldn't be out on a day like this! Besides, those folks are quarantined. Can't nobody go in there!"

"I've got to go, Bill! There's nobody to help them. They've got to eat. I promise I won't go in. I'm just going to leave this soup for them. Oh, please, Bill, please let me go."

"Well, I guess if you're crazy enough to want to go out in this storm, there's not much I can do to stop you. But you be careful now, hear?"

"Yes, yes, I will," she called, as she set off with her precious package held tightly on her lap, the good luck coin stuffed safely in her pocket. She rode as fast as she dared and reached the wooden bridge only to find the waters of the swollen river washing over the sides. Was it safe to cross? Would she and the horse be too heavy? She couldn't turn back now.

She eased her mount slowly toward the ramp. She could hear the bridge creak and groan over the sound of the roaring river, but it seemed to be holding. "Steady now," she called to the horse. "Easy does it."

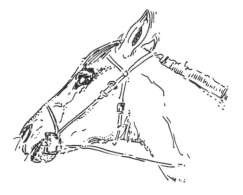

Lovina could hardly breathe. Her fear of water was still there, but she had something much more important to think about now. John needed her. She must hurry to him.

The horse sensed the danger as well, and whinnied fearfully with each tentative step. She was afraid he would bolt and turn back for home.

And then the horse refused to go on.

What should she do? Maybe if she let got off and led him across he would follow her. But what about the food? She'd just have to get the basket over first and then come back for the horse. Cross the river twice? How could she? But there was no other way.

She carefully slid from the saddle and backed the horse to a nearby tree. She looped the harness around a low branch and picked up the basket of food. The river was rising every minute. She knew she had no time to waste.

Lovina ran back to the bridge and stepped onto the wooden planks. She must be careful not to slip on the wet surface. Holding tightly to the railings, she held her breath and quickly ran to the other side. As soon as she placed the basket safely on the ground, she turned and made her way back to the frightened animal.

The horse was waiting, ears back, eyes wide. She loosened his harness and urged him on, "Steady boy, steady now."

At first the horse refused to move. She put her arm around his neck and began to speak softly into his ear. "Come on, boy, I need your help! You can do it! I know you can!" Lovina backed carefully onto the bridge, pulling the horse's harness with all her might. With nervous steps, the horse began to make his way slowly onto the bridge. They were just past half way when the bridge lurched suddenly.

"Oh, no," she prayed, "not now!"

A large tree had come tearing down the river and rammed against the railing. She heard a loud groan as the supports began to tear from the bridge pilings. Without hesitating, Lovina held onto the reins and ran quickly to the other side.

"Jump, boy! Jump!" she cried, and with one mighty leap, her horse cleared the gaping hole that was opening before him. The bridge gave a last tearing gasp and disappeared behind them into the raging river.

As Lovina watched in horror, her arms around the horse's

neck, she somehow knew that she had passed an important test in her life. She'd not only saved her horse, she had mastered her fear of water once and for all.

Now she must get to John. She climbed back onto the saddle and gently patted the horse's neck. "Good boy!" she whispered. "Now, let's go!"

When they reached the Cyrus' big house she dismounted and called up to the darkened window, "John, John! Can you hear me? Are you there John?"

At last she saw him. "Lovina, what are you...? You shouldn't be here," he whispered hoarsely.

"Nonsense. Here, take this!" she ordered, and passed the soup up to him. He smiled gratefully as he took the basket from her.

Lovina carried meals to John's family every day until the epidemic had passed. The trip took longer now that the bridge was out. The trail up the hill and through the cemetery was the only way to reach the Cyrus', but she never missed a day.

At the end of the two-week quarantine, John's father and two of his brothers had died, victims of the epidemic. Only John, his mother and sister had survived.

"How can we ever thank you, Vine?" he told her when he was well again. "I have my family to care for now, but I hope some day I can show you how much your help meant to us."

She smiled. "You know, John, I think I've helped myself more than you."

Lovina knew that her fears were finally gone—she could face whatever the future might bring.

On June 5th, 1855, John Cyrus and Lovina Graves were married. On the afternoon of their first wedding anniversary, John was waiting in the kitchen when Lovina returned from a neighborhood quilting party. What was he doing in the house at this time of day?

He took out his handkerchief and carefully blindfolded her. Then he took her by the hand and led her slowly into the parlor.

"What on earth are you doing, John?" she cried. She couldn't imagine what he was up to.

"Hush now. I have a little surprise for you," was all he would say.

"Now, John, what is all this?" When he removed the blindfold, she couldn't believe her eyes! There in front of

her was a brand new piano.

"Oh, John!" she cried. "Where did this come from?"

"I had it sent from San Francisco, Vine. I told you one time that I'd find a way to thank you, and here it is. I knew how much you loved your old piano, and this was the best present I could think of for my best girl."

"Oh, John! It's wonderful!" and she threw her arms around him.

Of course, the first tune she played was *Home Sweet Home.*

Epilogue

"I hope I've helped answer some of your questions, Emmy," said her grandmother as she finished her story.

Young Emmy was smiling. "Oh, yes, thank you, Grandmother. You were all heroes, you know. I'm so proud to be your granddaughter. But there is one more thing I'd like to know."

"What's that dear?" asked Lovina, her grandmother.

"Did Uncle Will ever find the coins your mother had hidden?"

"No he didn't, Emmy. In fact, there is more to the story of those coins. Nobody really believed us, you know. We were just children and no one thought we knew what we were talking about. Will searched all around for them, but he found nothing. We assumed they were gone forever.

"But some prospectors discovered those coins one day, some forty years later. They were buried between two rocks up near Donner Lake, just as our mother had said they'd be.

The men had heard the story of the lost treasure and knew right away who it belonged to; one of the coins even had teething marks on it from one of the babies. The dates stamped on the coins were right, and the location wasn't far from our cabin.

"We couldn't believe it when we saw them. Each of us in the family took some of the coins and we shared the rest with the men who found them. It was only fair.

"And now, Emmy," said Grandmother as she pulled her closer. "There's something I'd like you to have. Something I want you to carry with you, just as I did all those years ago. Maybe you'll have a granddaughter to give it to one day."

She reached into her apron pocket and pulled out a coin—a very, very old coin.

"Oh, Grandmother!" Emmy cried. "Is this the one…the one your mother gave you?"

"Yes, darling, the very one that brought me safely to California. And now it's your 'good-luck' coin—I wonder where it will take you?"

Bibliography

Archuleta, Kay. *Early Calistoga - The Brannan Saga.*
Illuminations Press, 1977.

Birney, Hoffman. *Grim Journey.* Minton, Bolch and
Co., 1934.

Ballantine, Betty and Ian, eds. *Native Americans, An
Illustrated History.* Turner Publishing Co., 1993.

Cushman, Karen. *The Ballad of Lucy Whipple.* Clarion
Books, Houghton Mifflin Co.,1996.

Elwell, Sharon. *Jeremy and the Wappo.* Rattle OK
Publications, 1991.

Gregory, Kristiana. *"Across the Wide and Lonesome
Prairie," Dear America.* Scholastic, Inc., 1997.

Johnson, Kristin. *Unfortunate Emigrants.* Utah State
University Press, 1996.

King, Joseph A. *Winter of Entrapment.* P. D. Meany
Publishers, 1993.

KQED Video. *The Donner Party,* 1995.

Laurgaard, Rachel. *Patty Reed's Doll.* Tomato
Enterprises, 1989.

Lavender, David. *Snowbound.* Holiday House, 1996.

Linse, Barbara with Kuska, George. *California's
Hispanic Roots For Kids.* Art's Publications, 1995.

Parkman, Francis. *The Oregon Trail.* Gramercy Books,
Random House Value Publishing, Inc., 1995.

Romtvedt, David. *Crossing Wyoming.* White Pine
Press, 1992.

Stewart, George R. *Ordeal by Hunger*. University of Nebraska Press, 1936.

Werner, Edna E. *Pioneer Children on the Journey West*. Westview Press, 1995.

Wright, Elizabeth Cyrus. *The Early Upper Napa Valley*. A Sharpsteen Museum Reprints Project, Barbara Neelands, ed., 1991.

About the Author
and the Illustrator

MARIAN RUDOLPH lives in Napa, California, where she was an elementary teacher and a Miller-Unruh reading specialist for over twenty years. She coordinated a parent education project at the Napa Adult School and is a popular storyteller. She has a Bachelor of Arts degree in Education from San Francisco State University and holds a Reading Specialist Teaching Credential. Marian and her husband, Ross, have five children, nine grandchildren, and a cocker spaniel named Chenin Blanc. *Lovina's Song* is her first book.

CHRISTOPHER COLE is a fifth generation Californian and a native of San Francisco. Since graduating from Humboldt State University in 1978, he has spent years exploring the fauna, flora and history of the California landscape. He now lives with his family in the Napa Valley, where he works as a professional land surveyor. His favorite tools include good boots, binoculars, a garden trowel, pen, paper and brush.

HOME! SWEET HOME!

Music by Henry Bishop, Lyrics by John Howard Payne, 1823.

ANDANTE.

'Mid__ plea - ures and pal - ac - es though we may roam, Be it ev - er so hum - ble, there's no place like home. A charm from the skies seems to hal - low us there, which

seek thro' the world is ne'er met with else-where.

Home! Home! Sweet, sweet home! There's no place like

home, There's no place like home.

An exile from home, splendor dazzles in vain,
Oh, give me my lowly thatched cottage again.
The birds singing gaily, that came at my call,
Give me them with that piece of mind,
dearer than all.

To thee, I'll return, overburdened with care,
The heart's dearest solace will smile on me there.
No more from that cottage again will I roam,
Be it ever so humble,
there's no place like home.

Such is the patriot's boast, wher'er we roam,
His first, best country ever is at home.
– Oliver Goldsmith

ORDER DIRECTLY FROM CITRON BAY

LOVINA'S SONG A PIONEER GIRL'S JOURNEY WITH THE DONNER PARTY
BY MARIAN RUDOLPH

$11.95

TEACHER'S RESOURCE GUIDE

$14.95

for *Lovina's Song*

Contains many ideas and activities to enrich student's learning and expand understanding of history and social studies, as well as language arts, science, mathematics, art, and music. Designed around the California Department of Education's curriculum requirements.

CLASSROOM SET—24 *Lovina's Song* Books with *Teacher's Resource Guide*

$168.00

SING WITH ME ABC (WITH MUSIC CD)

$16.95

BY BENTE MARTINSEN & SOLVEIG PEDERSEN

A fun way for children ages 4 to 7 to learn the alphabet and discover reading. Great songs! Excellent learning tool for preschool, kindergarten, and first grade. Includes: Music CD, Student Workbook and Teacher's Guide with sheet music.

Makes a wonderful gift for an individual student too!

CLASSROOM SET—24 Student Workbooks for *Sing With Me ABC*

$59.95

California residents add 7.50%. Add $3.50 for shipping. Send your order with delivery address and check or school purchase order to:

Citron Bay Orders
77 Windstone Dr. Suite #103
San Rafael, CA 94903
(415) 472-1208
www.citronbay.com